ABSTRACTED MORTALITY SCHEDULE

Florida State Census of 1885

Alvie L. Davidson, CG

HERITAGE BOOKS
2014

HERITAGE BOOKS
AN IMPRINT OF HERITAGE BOOKS, INC.

Books, CDs, and more—Worldwide

For our listing of thousands of titles see our website
at
www.HeritageBooks.com

Published 2014 by
HERITAGE BOOKS, INC.
Publishing Division
5810 Ruatan Street
Berwyn Heights, Md. 20740

Heritage Books by the author:

Abstracted Mortality Schedule, Florida State Census of 1885

*Florida Land: Records of the Tallahassee and
Newnansville General Land Office, 1825–1892*

International Standard Book Numbers
Paperbound: 978-0-7884-3716-8
Clothbound: 978-0-7884-9040-8

1885 Florida State Census

Mortality Schedule

This is an effort to abstract from the surviving county census records of this fairly unique census which covered manufacturing, agriculture, and mortality enumerations. The following information reveals why there will be no mortality schedules for four of the counties in existence at that time.

This abstract has the name, age, sex, race, birthplace of individual and both parents, month of the death, cause of death (where shown) and name of physician (where shown).

The index is a separate part of this work and can be found in the back of this work. My wife and I worked on this for many, many hours. The actual census pages were copied from the holdings of the Tampa Public Library where the census is on microfilm. Next they were printed in paper copy for easier reading.

"The 1885 state census was partially funded by the Federal government. Questions asked were to reflect the individual's status as of 1 June 1885. While the 1885 census included population, agriculture, manufactures, and mortality schedules, this database contains only the population schedules. Thirty-five of the thirty-nine Florida counties are included here. Only Alachua, Clay, Columbia, and Nassau are excluded because they appear to be missing from NARA's copies.

Microfilmed copies of this census are held at the National Archives and the LDS Family History Library. The 1890 U.S. Federal Census was damaged and destroyed by fire in 1921. Less than 1% of the schedules are available for research today. Because of this problem, the 1885 Florida State Census has become a highly valuable source, as it provides a wealth of information that would otherwise be found in the Federal Census.

State censuses were often taken in years between the federal censuses. In some places, local censuses were designed to collect specific data, such as the financial strengths and needs of communities; tallies of school-age children and potential school populations to predict needs for teachers and facilities; censuses of military strength, cavalry horse resources, and grain storage; enumeration for revenue assessment and urban planning; and lists to monitor African Americans moving into the northern cities."

Taken from Szucs, Loretto Dennis, "Research in Census Records." In *The Source: A Guidebook of American Genealogy,* ed. Loretto Dennis Szucs and Sandra Hargreaves Luebking (Salt Lake City: Ancestry, 1997).

Alvie L. Davidson CG
Dianne Hatcher Davidson
4825 N. Galloway Road
Lakeland, Florida 33810   18 August 2008

PONS, Mary; 16; F; White; FL; FL; FL; - ; Sept; - ; Baker

PARKER, Orvil L.; 1; M; White; FL; FL; FL; - ; Nov; sudden;
Baker

COBB, Lena A.; - ; F; White; FL; FL; GA; - ; March; Hives;
Baker

DRIGGER, Martha; 24; F; White; FL; GA; GA; Housework;
August; Dropsy; Baker

NEWMANS, Mary; 1; F; White; FL; GA; FL; - ; August; Brain
Fever; Baker

NEWMANS, Millie L.; 5; F; White; FL; GA; FL; - ; August;
Brain Fever; Baker

SHEELS, Walter D.; 2; M; White; FL; ENG; FL; - ; July; Chronic
Diarrhea; Baker

BURNSED, James M.; 72; M; White; GA; - ; GA; Farmer; April;
Pneumonia; Baker

RANLESSER, Thomas; 1; M; White; FL; FL; GA; - ; Dec;
Chronic Diarrhea; Baker

HARVEY (?), Linnie; 7; F; White; FL; GA; FL; - ; Nov; Heart
Disease; Baker

COOPER, Thomas; 7; M; White; FL; GA; FL; - ; Jan; Pneumonia;
Baker

STRICKLAND, Mrs. Mary; 65; F; White; GA; GA; GA;
Housework; Dec; Pneumonia; Baker

CHAMBERS, Mrs. Cassie; 21; F; White; FL; NC; GA;
Housework; Nov; Dropsy; Baker

BERRY, Levi; 35; M; White; NH; - ; - ; Farmer; May; Typhoid
Fever; Baker

EDWARDS, Ivan; - ; M; White; FL; IN; IA; - ; May; Cholera
Infection; Baker

HICKS, Eliza; 1; F; White; FL; FL; FL; - ; June; - ; Baker

WYMAN, C. W.; 70; M; White; NS; - ; CT; Farmer; Nov;
Paralysis; Bradford

MUDGE, S. F.; 64; F; White; MA; - ; - ; - ; Aug; Dropsy;
Bradford

SPARKMAN, C.; 36; F; White; FL; FL; FL; - ; Mar; Heart
Disease; Bradford

HALL, Rosa; 25; F; Black; FL; Fl; FL; Housework; Jan; Heart
   Disease; Bradford
MILLS, W. W.; 58; M; White; PA; PA; PA; Lawyer; Sept;
   Essethelimoa(?); Bradford
MARTEN, W. L.; 21; M; White; KY; KY; MO; Salesman; May;
   Lung Disease; Bradford
RENNOLS, Mary; 37; F; Black; FL; FL; FL; Housework; July;
   Dropsy; Bradford
UNDERHILL, Jerry; 1; M; White; FL; FL; FL; - ; May; Teething;
   Bradford
PALMER, Elizabeth; 84; F; White; GA; GA; GA; Pauper; Aug;
   Unknown; Bradford
THOMAS, Annie E.; 1; F; White; FL; FL; FL; - ; - ; Congestion
   lungs; Bradford
McCREA, M. L.; 66; M; White; SC; SC; SC; Pauper; May;
   Overdose Drug; Bradford
RIMES, Mary; 68; F; White; GA; GA; GA; - ; June;
   Consumption; Bradford
HAYES, Ben; 3; M; White; FL; FL; FL; - ; Sept; Dropsy;
   Bradford
HAYES, Fred; 2; M; White; FL; FL; FL; - ; Sept; Dropsy;
   Bradford
DOUGLAS, Victoria; 35; F; White; FL; GA; GA; - ; April;
   Burned; Bradford
DOUGLAS, Cora; 20; F; White; FL; FL; - ; - ; Nov; Pleurisy;
   Bradford
SHELL, William; 9; M; White; GA; GA; GA; - ; July; Congestion
   brain; Bradford
GROVNER, Joshua; 87; M; White; FL; FL; GA; Farmer; Nov;
   Unknown; Bradford
KASC, Ola; 1; F; White; FL; GA; FL; - ; Sept; Teething; Bradford
FOGEL, C; 1; M; White; FL; SC; SC; - ; Aug; Worms/Cholic;
   Bradford
SYKES, M. A.; 50; F; White; GA; NC; NC; - ; Feb; Neuralgia;
   Bradford
HODGES, E. E.; 26; M; White; GA; NC; GA; Farmer; May; Brain
   Fever; Bradford

JOHN, Jerry; 45; M; White; FL; - ; - ; - ; June; Bowl
Inflammation; Bradford

FOWLER, Eliza; 48; F; White; FL; NC; GA; - ; Aug; Malaria;
Bradford

SMITH, John; 42; M; White; Ireland; Ireland; Ireland; Ditcher;
Sept; Brain Paralysis; Bradford

Infant; 0; M; White; FL; GA; FL; - ; Dec; Thrash; Bradford

SHAW, Jacob M.; 5; M; White; FL; FL; FL; - ; Sept; Scalded;
Bradford

WILLIS, B.; 11; M; White; FL; GA; GA; - ; Sept; Heart
Inflammation; Bradford

REDDISH, Jack; 54; M; White; GA; GA; GA; Farmer; March;
Congestion bowels; Bradford

WEBB, Lettie; 1; F; White; FL; GA; GA; - ; April; Congestion
bowels; Bradford

RAHENE, J. C.; 22; M; White; PA; Germany; Germany; Farmer;
Jan; Pneumonia; Bradford

ALBERT, H.; 23; F; Black; FL; GA; GA; - ; July; Fever; Bradford

JONES, M. M.; 18; F; Black; GA; GA; GA; - ; July; Typhoid
Fever; Bradford

GEIGER, John; 8; M; White; FL; FL; FL; - ; July; Congestion
bowels; Bradford

WILKINSON, J. N.; 40; M; White; VA; ENG; VA; Merchant;
Dec; Chronic Diarrhea; Brevard

DANIEL, E. C. J.; 23; M; White; MA; MA; MA; Boatman; Dec;
Drowned; Brevard

PULOW, Jesse; 58; M; White; NY; - ; - ; Farmer; Dec; Apoplexy;
Brevard

BROWN, J. A.; 50; M; White; NY; - ; - ; MD; May;
Consumption; Brevard

HALL, Hiram; 75; M; White; GA; GA; GA; Farmer; Dec;
Paralysis; Brevard

CHINA, G. G.; 26; F; White; GA; Scotland; GA; Housewife; Jan;
Consumption; Brevard

GRAY, Daniel; 69; M; White; NY; Canada; NY; Lawyer; Jan;
Consumption; Brevard

CHAPPELL, Gracie; 2; F; White; FL; NY; GA; - ; July; Brain
Fever; Brevard

Name; Age; Sex; Race; Born; FABorn; MOBorn;
          Occup; DODeath; Cause Of Death; County

THOMAS, Jas.; 23; M; White; FL; GA; GA; Merchant; Nov;
    Throat Cut; Brevard
McCRORY, Nina; 19; F; White; GA; GA; GA; Housewife; Nov;
    Enteritis; Brevard
HOOK, Hendrick; 1; M; White; AL; GA; AL; - ; July; Dysentery;
    Brevard
MCMULLAN, A. A.; 6; M; White; FL; NC; FL; - ; April;
    Congestion Brain; Brevard
SHEFFIELD, James; 1; M; White; FL; WI; WI; - ; Oct; Inflam.
    Bowel; Brevard
MORGAN, Dozier; 18; M; White; FL; GA; GA; Stock Raise; Feb;
    Acc. Gun Shot; Brevard
BRENNAN, Edw.; 2; M; White; FL; FL; FL; - ; March; Cho.
    Inflam.; Brevard
BRENNAN, Florence; 4; F; White; FL; FL; FL; - ; Dec; Cho.
    Inflam.; Brevard
BRENNAN, James; 8; M; White; FL; FL; FL; - ; March; Cho.
    Inflam.; Brevard
HAIR, Harlis; 5; M; White; FL; FL; FL; - ; Oct; Dropsy; Brevard
YATES, Jackson; 1; M; White; FL; FL; FL; - ; June; Acc. Burned;
    Brevard
TUMBLIN, Hardy; 52; M; White; GA; GA; GA; Farmer; Feb;
    Pneumonia; Brevard
SMITH, Infant; 1; M; White; FL; FL; AL; - ; - ; Deformed/idiot;
    Calhoun
STONE, J. E.; 14; M; White; FL; FL; FL; - ; Oct; Fall; Calhoun
STONE, Mary; 12; F; White; FL; FL; FL; - ; Oct; Dropsy;
    Calhoun
STONE, Hattie; 3; F; White; FL; FL; FL; - ; June; Cong. Brain;
    Calhoun
AYERS, Winnie; 27; F; White; FL; FL; SC; - ; May; Dropsy;
    Calhoun
WOOD, Lollie S.; 3; F; White; FL; FL; GA; - ; April; Congestion;
    Calhoun
WOOD, Paul; 1; M; White; FL; FL; GA; - ; May; Unknown;
    Calhoun
WOOD, May P.; 1; F; White; FL; FL; GA; - ; May; Unknown;
    Calhoun

BARFIELD, Frank; 12; M; White; FL; AL; FL; - ; April;
Accidentally killed; Calhoun

AYERS, Josie; 27; F; White; FL; GA; FL; - ; Mar; Dropsy;
Calhoun

MORRIS, Samantha; 9; F; White; FL; GA; FL; - ; Nov; Dropsy;
Calhoun

REUSS, Martha; 37; F; White; FL; AL; AL; - ; May; Dropsy;
Calhoun

SMITH, R. L.; 58; M; White; NC; NC; NC; Orange Gr.; Nov;
Unknown; Calhoun

KING, Elvina; 46; F; Black; FL; GA; FL; Cook; Jan;
Consumption; Duval

BUSH, Eddie; 1; F; Black; FL; - ; - ; - ; Feb; Fever; Duval

NAMES MISSING; 75; M; Black; SC; - ; - ; Laborer; - ;
Unknown; Duval

BUTLER, Jane; 47; F; White; GA; SC; SC; - ; Aug; Dropsy;
Duval

ENGLISH, Rehina; 1; F; Black; FL; FL; FL; - ; March; Yellow
Thrash; Duval

INENT, Illa; 2; F; Mu; FL; - ; AL; - ; June; Pneumonia; Duval

SAMON, James; 65; M; Black; SC; SC; SC; Laborer; Nov;
Consumption; Duval

REDDISH, Moses; 58; M; Black; NC; - ; - ; Brk. Mason; Dec;
Consumption; Duval

BODEN, Lottie; 1; F; White; FL; ENG; SC; - ; June; Cholera
Infection; Duval

BALL, Sarah; 70; F; White; Mer (?); VA; Mer (?); - ; March; Old
Age; Duval

GARMIN, Wilemina; 3; F; Mu; FL; FL; FL; - ; Nov; Brain Fever;
Duval

GIBSON, Lula; 1; F; Black; FL; Mer(?); FL; - ; July; Spasms;
Duval

CHAMBERS, George; 78; M; Black; SC; SC; SC; Laborer; June;
Explosion; Duval

WILLIAMS, Johnny; 1; M; Black; FL; FL; FL; - ; May; Teething;
Duval

MURRAY, Florence; 3; F; White; VA; Canada; VA; - ; Aug;
Dysentery; Duval

Name; Age; Sex; Race; Born; FABorn; MOBorn; Occup; DODeath; Cause Of Death; County

HARRISON, William; 16; M; Black; FL; GA; FL; Cigar Maker; April; Burroughs; Duval

HART, Ely; 60; M; Black; SC; SC; SC; Brk.Mason; Aug; Pneumonia; Duval

BROOKS, Ansy; 1; M; Black; FL; FL; FL; - ; Sept; Diarrhea; Duval

HUDSON, Wm. G.; 1; M; Black; FL; NC; FL; - ; - ; Unknown; Duval

WILLIAMS, Chas.; 2; M; Black; GA; FL; FL; - ; - ; Unknown; Duval

WALTNER, Frank (?); 27; M; White; NY; NY; NY; Cigar Maker; March; Consumption; Duval

CLARK, Charlotte; 30; F; Black; FL; FL; FL; - ; Oct; Consumption; Duval

THOMPSON, Harry; 32; M; Black; SC; SC; SC; - ; May; Consumption; Duval

SMITHAL (?), Jennie; 102; F; Black; VA; VA; VA; Cook; - ; Old Age; Duval

NELSON, Louisa; 1; F; Black; FL; FL; FL; - ; June; - ; Duval

SANCHES, Edward; 34; M; Black; SC; FL; FL; - ; March; - ; Duval

GITHENS, Florence; 18; F; White; FL; FL; FL; - ; Jan; Consumption; Duval

GEIGER, Louis; 14; M; White; FL; FL; FL; - ; Oct; Congestion bowels; Duval

GARDNER, E.; 72; F; White; FL; FL; FL; - ; Sept; Old Age; Duval

CHALMERS, E.; 27; F; White; Scotland; Scotland; Scotland; Laundry; March; Congestive chill; Duval

HENDERSON, H. E.; 40; F; White; FL; FL; FL; - ; Feb; Inflam. bowels; Duval

ROACH, J. P.; 1; M; White; FL; FL; FL; - ; Mar; Inflam. bowels; Duval

HAGIN, Ophelia; 1; F; Black; FL; FL; FL; - ; Oct; Inflam. Bowels; Duval

WEMHILL, E.; 55; M; Black; NC; NC; NC; Stevedore; May; Dropsy; Duval

FERRELL, M.; 30; F; White; FL; GA; GA; Seamstress; May;
Dropsy; Duval

GILLEN, M; 84; F; White; NC; - ; NC; Seamstress; Jan;
Pneumonia; Duval

CASON, W. H.; 8; M; White; FL; GA; GA; - ; Oct; Dropsy;
Duval

WALKER, Alfred; 1; M; Black; FL; FL; FL; - ; May; Premature
Birth; Duval

BRYAN, Thos.; 40; M; White; ENG; ENG; ENG; - ; Jan;
Consumption; Duval

LOYD, Tammy; 1; F; White; FL; GA; SC; - ; Nov; Teething;
Duval

LOYD, Baby; 1; F; White; FL; GA; SC; - ; April; Premature
Birth; Duval

SMITH, Halliday; 20; M; White; FL; GA; SC; Jeweller; Oct;
Drowned; Duval

ROBINSON, Lizzie; 30; F; White; FL; FL; FL; - ; May;
Unknown; Duval

DOSSING, F.; 30; F; White; GER; Germany; Germany; Baker;
June; Unknown; Duval

CROSBY, Frank; 26; M; Black; GA; GA; GA; Laborer; June;
Unknown; Duval

LANGNORD, Hugh; 30; M; White; GER; GER; GER; Laborer;
June; Unknown; Duval

BETHEL, Teresa; 21; F; Black; GA; GA; GA; Servant; July;
Unknown; Duval

GILLIAN, Henrietta; 65; F; Black; SC; SC; SC; - ; Aug;
Unknown; Duval

BULLOCK, Lucy; 35; F; Black; GA; GA; GA; - ; Aug; Unknown;
Duval

CALMS (?), Jacob; 70; M; Black; FL; FL; FL; - ; Nov; Unknown;
Duval

MURPHY, Matthew; 28; M; White; FL; FL; FL; - ; Nov;
Unknown; Duval

DEAR, Alfred; 35; M; Black; SC; SC; SC; - ; Nov; Unknown;
Duval

AULY (?), Terin(?); 35; M; Black; FL; FL; FL; - ; Nov;
Unknown; Duval

Name; Age; Sex; Race; Born; FABorn; MOBorn;
Occup; DODeath; Cause Of Death; County

PRICE, Jas.; 83; M; White; NY; NY; NY; - ; Sept; Unknown;
Duval

BAKER, Wm.; 28; M; Black; FL; FL; FL; - ; Sept; Unknown;
Duval

DICKSON, Joe; 40; M; Black; FL; FL; FL; - ; Sept; Unknown;
Duval

HYDER, Wm.; 65; M; Black; SC; SC; SC; - ; Oct; Unknown;
Duval

LOUIS, R.; 32; M; Black; SC; SC; SC; - ; Oct; Unknown; Duval

MILES, Ed.; 69; M; Black; SC; SC; SC; - ; Oct; Unknown; Duval

FENDWICK, Ed.; 17; M; White; FL; FL; FL; - ; Oct; Unknown;
Duval

FAIRBY, Blossie; 1; F; Mu; FL; FL; FL; - ; May; Teething; Duval

ANDREWS, Marie; 1; F; White; FL; FL; FL; - ; Nov; Premature
Birth; Duval

GILCHRIST, Geo. D.; 45; M; White; NY; - ; - ; Lumber; May;
Congestion liver; Duval

KAVENY, Kate; 83; F; White; Ireland; FL; FL; Servant; March;
Consumption; Duval

PAYNE, Ellen; 45; F; White; NY; VA; CT; - ; Oct; Heart Disease;
Duval

RICHE, Clymentina; 5; F; White; FL; MS; FL; - ; Nov; Capillary
[?]; Duval

BUNDY, ?; 38; F; Black; TN; - ; - ; Cook; - ; Unknown; Duval

ADDISON, Larinia; 1; F; Black; FL; FL; - ; - ; Sept; Diarrhea;
Duval

KINGSTON, Arthir; 65; M; White; Ireland; Ireland; Ireland; - ;
Nov; Unknown; Duval

VENDICK, Chas.; 24; M; White; Norway; Norway; Norway;
Sailor; May; Consumption; Duval

WALKER, Mabel; 1; F; White; FL; SC; AL; - ; - ; Water on
Brain; Duval

HALL, Sophie; 79; F; Black; GA; - ; - ; - ; May; Heart; Duval

WALL, L. W.; 50; M; White; GA; - ; - ; Contractor; - ;
Cancer/stomach; Duval

RUSSELL, Ella; 23; F; White; GA; - ; - ; - ; March; Consumption;
Duval

WILLIAMS, J. L.; 51; M; White; Germany; - ; - ; - ; Feb; - ;
Duval

MEEGAN, Jas.; 72; M; White; Ireland; Ireland; Ireland; Librarian;
March; Congestive chill; Duval

ROBINSON, Patsy; 60; F; Black; SC; - ; - ; - ; June; Paralysis;
Duval

LANDIN, Nellie; 37; M; White; PA; - ; - ; - ; June; Paralysis;
Duval

POMOROY, Benj.; 41; M; Mu; FL; FL; FL; Fisherman; Jan;
Consumption; Duval

FLEMING, Lorrain; 56; F; Mu; FL; FL; GA; - ; Feb; Pneumonia;
Duval

ADAMS, Fred; 1; M; Black; FL; FL; FL; - ; May; Pneumonia;
Duval

SARGENT, Adam; 4; M; Black; FL; FL; GA; - ; May;
Accidentally shot; Duval

HIGGINBOTHAM, Elizabeth; 56; F; White; FL; FL; FL; - ; June;
Paralysis; Duval

MURRAY, Florence; 24; F; Black; FL; AL; AL; - ; Nov;
Consumption; Duval

SPRINGLETON, Clara; 1; F; Black; FL; FL; FL; - ; June;
Teething; Duval

SPRINGLETON, Lawrence; 1; M; Black; FL; FL; FL; - ; April;
Lung Disease; Duval

MURRAY, Louisa; 1; F; Black; FL; FL; FL; - ; April; Pneumonia;
Duval

JOHNSON, Isaac; 1; M; Black; FL; - ; FL; - ; May; Inward Piles;
Duval

JOHNSON, Elizabeth; 24; F; White; FL; GA; FL; - ; April; Child
Birth; Duval

WILLIAMS, Florinda; 24; F; White; FL; FL; FL; - ; Nov;
Consumption; Duval

NAPLAIN (?), Mary; - ; F; Black; FL; FL; FL; - ; Sept; Unknown;
Duval

YOUNG, Lily; 2; F; Black; FL; GA; FL; - ; Oct; Fever; Duval

MITCHELL, Clarissa; 28; F; Black; FL; GA; FL; - ; April;
Consumption; Duval

BROWN, J.; 35; M; White; FL; GA; FL; - ; May; Unknown; Duval

HILL, Jno.; 44; M; White; FL; GA; FL; - ; May; Unknown; Duval

THORNTON, O. A.; 50; M; White; MD; MD; MD; - ; May; Unknown; Duval

DUBOIS, Louis P.; 29; M; White; NY; NY; Canada; - ; Dec; Paralysis; Duval

FULLER, Joseph; 1; M; Black; FL; NC; NC; - ; April; Cholera Infection; Duval

STEWARD, Louisa; 33; F; Black; FL; AL; AL; - ; May; Heart Disease; Duval

MATHEWS, Fla; 1; F; Mu; FL; SC; SC; - ; Nov; Cholera Infection; Duval

KENNARD, N. Y.; 18; F; Black; FL; SC; SC; Nurse; Nov; Sore Throat; Duval

LAKEMAN (?), Anthony; 18; F; White; FL; FL; FL; - ; March; Bilious Fever; Duval

FERNANDEZ, E. L.; 40; F; Black; FL; FL; FL; - ; Dec; Consumption; Duval

WILLIAMS, Willie; 1; M; Black; FL; SC; SC; - ; March; Teething; Duval

FORBS, Mary; 1; F; Mu; FL; FL; FL; - ; Feb; Pneumonia; Duval

DIX, Daniel; 27; M; Mu; LA; VA; OH; Porter; Dec; Bright's Disease; Duval

CURTIS, Milton; 1; M; Black; FL; AL; FL; - ; Oct; Unknown; Duval

HEMPS, M. E. E.; 35; F; Black; NC; NC; NC; - ; March; Heart Disease; Duval

CHAPPLE, A. G.; 45; M; White; RI; RI; RI; Ship Joiner; May; Accident; Duval

SWAIN, Thos. T.; 53; M; White; NJ; NJ; NJ; Jeweler; Oct; Bright's Disease; Duval

KERNAN, Wm. A.; 40; M; White; PA; Ireland; France; Carpenter; May; Consumption; Duval

FERRIEA, Eugenia; 23; F; White; FL; FL; FL; - ; Mar; Jaundice; Duval

THOMPSON, Isa B.; 5; F; White; FL; MD; FL; - ; May; Measles; Duval

HOLMES, Alice D.; 19; F; White; NC; NC; NC; - ; May; Bilious
Fever; Duval

BOYD, A. M.; 3; F; White; FL; MD; NJ; - ; Nov; Unknown;
Duval

BOYD, Allice; 10; F; White; NY; - ; Ireland; - ; Oct; Dingie
Fever; Duval

GARVIN, N. C.; 5; F; Mu; FL; W.I.; GA; - ; May; Measles; Duval

HUNTER, Frank; 13; F; Black; FL; FL; FL; - ; July; Dysentery;
Duval

GARNETT, M. A.; 30; M; White; VA; VA; VA; Real Estate;
April; Diabetes; Duval

GARNETT, M. A.; 36; F; White; FL; Scotland; GA; - ; Oct; Child
Birth; Duval

GORDEN, E.; 61; M; White; GA; GA; GA; - ; March;
Consumption; Duval

ROBINSON, M. M.; 2; F; White; NC; NC; NC; - ; May; Bilious
Fever; Duval

ANTHONY, Meyer; 35; M; Black; GA; NC; NC; Laborer; April;
Old Age; Duval

CASTLE, Mary F.; 1; F; White; FL; FL; FL; - ; Oct; Brain Fever;
Duval

WILLIAMS, Jnoy.; 40; F; Black; SC; SC; SC; - ; April; Heart
Disease; Duval

COPLEY, Hallie; 1; F; Mu; FL; IL; IL; - ; Dec; Interm. Fever;
Duval

WIGHTMAN, Wm.; 1; M; White; FL; SC; NY; - ; June; Teething;
Duval

LAWSON, Lue; 37; F; Black; GA; SC; VA; - ; June;
Consumption; Duval

RICHARDSON, Jas.; 1; M; Mu; AL; AL; AL; - ; May; Fever;
Duval

DAVIS, Albert; 1; F; Mu; FL; FL; FL; - ; May; Fever; Duval

POINSETT, C. M.; 70; F; White; FL; NY; NY; - ; April; Fever;
Duval

WILLIAMS, Francis; 3; F; Black; FL; FL; FL; - ; May; Fever;
Duval

FARMER, Jas.; 19; M; Black; FL; FL; FL; - ; Feb; Unknown;
Duval

BROWN, Ellen; 34; F; White; FL; FL; GA; - ; May; Typhoid
    Fever; Duval
SKINNER, Laura; 2; F; White; FL; FL; GA; - ; April;
    Menningitis; Duval
OWENS, Emma; 2; F; White; FL; FL; FL; - ; June; Spinal; Duval
MATHEWS, Jno.; 1; M; White; FL; FL; FL; - ; June; Fever;
    Duval
WEST, I [unreadable]; 4; F; White; FL; FL; FL; - ; Feb;
    Consumption; Duval
GETCHEL, Mrs.; 56; F; White; ENG; ENG; ENG; - ; Jan; Heart
    Disease; Duval
WETMORE, Frank; 1; M; White; FL; FL; FL; - ; Jan; Throat;
    Duval
TURNER, Frank; 31; M; White; FL; FL; FL; - ; Mar;
    Consumption; Duval
HAMILTON, Geo. W.; 6; M; Colored; FL; FL; FL; - ; Mar; Gen.
    Debility; Duval
ALSPAUGH, Mrs.; 50; F; White; FL; FL; FL; - ; Mar; Unknown;
    Duval
THOMPSON, Bertha; 1; F; Colored; FL; VA; FL; - ; June;
    Thrash; Duval
THOMAS, Baby; 1; M; Colored; FL; FL; FL; - ; Mar; Unknown;
    Duval
WEST, Lige; 38; M; White; GA; GA; GA; - ; June; Kidney; Duval
WALDEN, Chas.; 10; M; White; NC; NC; NC; - ; May; Bilious
    Fever; Duval
WALDEN, Joe; 8; M; White; NC; NC; NC; - ; June; Bilious
    Fever; Duval
MILLER, V.; 4; F; Colored; FL; FL; FL; - ; July; Fever; Duval
WILLIAMS, Jno.; 52; M; White; ENG; ENG; ENG; Pile Driver;
    Aug; Killed; Duval
CANOVA, Vic; 38; F; White; FL; FL; F; - ; Mar; Consumption;
    Duval
HINSON, Rose; 1; F; White; MI; MI; MI; - ; April; Cholera
    Infection; Duval
WHITE, Ed; 45; M; Colored; VA; VA; VA; Carpenter; Jan;
    Paralysis; Duval

BUTLER, S. F.; 41; M; Colored; NP; NP; NC; Cigar Maker; Oct;
Chills & Fever; Duval
RICHAN, Francis; 34; M; Colored; FL; FL; FL; Carpenter; Feb;
Consumption; Duval
HOLLAND, Leone; 26; F; Colored; FL; FL; FL; - ; Feb;
Consumption; Duval
RICHAN, Ella; 25; F; Colored; FL; FL; FL; - ; June;
Consumption; Duval
BARNS, W.; 1; M; Colored; FL; FL; Fl; - ; April; Unknown;
Duval
ANDERSON, E.; 1; F; Colored; FL; FL; FL; - ; July; Unknown;
Duval
RANEY, L.; 1; F; Colored; GA; GA; GA; - ; April; Killed by [?];
Duval
WILLIAMS, Liza; 1; F; Colored; FL; SC; FL; - ; April; Unknown;
Duval
MILLER, Hattie; 10; F; Colored; FL; SC; SC; - ; Feb;
Consumption; Duval
GOODWIN, H.; 6; F; Colored; FL; FL; FL; - ; June; Unknown;
Duval
EDWARDS, L.; 1; M; Colored; FL; FL; FL; - ; June; Unknown;
Duval
SPICER, Geo.; 1; M; Colored; FL; FL; FL; - ; Dec; Unknown;
Duval
JINKINS, Kate; 24; F; Colored; FL; FL; SC; - ; June; Unknown;
Duval
GREEN, Joe; 1; M; Colored; FL; LA; GA; - ; June; Diarrhea;
Duval
MILLER, U. U.; 1; M; White; NY; NY; NY; - ; June;
Consumption; Duval
GIBBONS, Lock; 10; M; White; IL; NY; OH; - ; Dec; Unknown;
Duval
FARMER, Jas.; 25; M; Black; GA; GA; GA; - ; Feb; Unknown;
Duval
ENGLISH, Mary; 35; F; White; FL; GA; GA; Homemaker; Aug;
Consumption; Duval
CASEY, Kate; 22; F; Black; FL; FL; FL; Seamstress; Sept;
Malarial Fever; Duval

BUTLER, Rebecca; 54; F; White; FL; FL; FL; Homemaker; June;
    Inflam. bowels; Duval
PELOT, Burt; 32; M; Black; FL; FL; FL; Laborer; July;
    Pneumonia; Duval
PELOT, Mary; 2; F; Black; FL; FL; FL; - ; Sept; - ; Duval
WAGNER, Frank; 28; M; Black; FL; VA; GA; - ; Oct;
    Consumption; Duval
ANDREWS, Maggie; 1; F; White; FL; SC; SC; - ; May;
    Pneumonia; Duval
BROWN, Lewis; 34; M; Black; VL; GA; GA; Laborer; Sept;
    Consumption; Duval
COOK, Minnie; - ; F; White; FL; FL; FL; - ; Feb; Pneumonia;
    Duval
RICHARDSON, Geo.; 42; M; White; FL; GA; GA; - ; Oct;
    Bilious Fever; Duval
GRANT, Jno. L.; 18; M; Black; FL; FL; FL; Newsboy; Oct;
    Killed; Duval
JONES, Chas.; 20; M; White; FL; FL; FL; Laborer; Dec;
    Pneumonia; Duval
DOWLING, David; 18; M; White; FL; FL; FL; Newsboy; Jan;
    Congestion Brain; Duval
DOWLING, Clarence; 2; M; White; FL; FL; FL; - ; April;
    Congestion Brain; Duval
COOPER, Mary; 17; F; White; FL; GA; GA; Seamstress; - ;
    Dropsy; Duval
BRYANT, Tms.; 1; M; White; FL; FL; FL; - ; Aug; Worms;
    Duval
WIGGINS, Glasco; 107; M; Black; SC; SC; SC; Minister; Feb;
    Old Age; Duval
LAND, Jno.; 63; M; Black; FL; FL; FL; Car Greaser; Dec; Killed;
    Duval
WHITE, Wm.; 3; M; White; FL; FL; FL; - ; Mar; Worms; Duval
EVANS, Henrietta; 1; F; White; FL; FL; FL; - ; Feb; Pneumonia;
    Duval
HILL, Etta; 1; F; White; FL; FL; GA; - ; July; Unknown; Duval
DAVIS, Dock; 15; M; Black; FL; FL; FL; Laborer; Aug;
    Unknown; Duval

DAVIS, Margaret; 19; F; Black; FL; FL; FL; Washing; Sept;
Child Birth; Duval

HANDY, Ellen; 1; F; Black; FL; GA; FL; - ; May; Pneumonia;
Duval

F[-----], Israel; 3; M; White; FL; GA; GA; - ; Oct; Pneumonia;
Duval

SALIMON, Annis; 1; M; Black; FL; NC; SC; - ; April; Malaria;
Duval

WHITE, Adam; 65; M; White; NC; NC; NC; Brick Man; Aug;
Diarrhea; Duval

WILSON, Abram; 1; M; Black; NC; FL; FL; - ; Sept; Nettle Rash;
Duval

McRAE, Sallie; 46; F; White; SC; SC; SC; Washing; Oct; Brain
Fever; Duval

THOMPSON, Louis; 12; M; Black; FL; NC; SC; Newsboy; May;
Menningitis; Duval

CLARK, Wm.; 74; M; Black; SC; VA; VA; Butcher; Oct;
Mashed; Duval

CLARK, Wm.; 1; M; Black; FL; FL; FL; - ; Sept; Worms; Duval

WATSON, Lula; 19; F; White; FL; FL; FL; Seamstress; Dec;
Menningitis; Duval

McDONALD, N.; 40; F; White; FL; FL; FL; - ; Oct; Unknown;
Duval

SULLIVAN, D. F.; 47; M; White; Ireland; Ireland; Ireland;
Mechanic; June; Apoplexy; Escambia

WHEELER, D. T.; 8; M; White; FL; Ireland; Ireland; - ; May;
Unknown; Escambia

THOMAS, Wm.; 40; M; Black; AL; AL; AL; Laborer; March;
Pneumonia; Escambia

CARMICHAIL, M.; 23; F; White; FL; FL; AL; - ; March;
Typhoid Fever; Escambia

SEARL, Agnes; 80; F; Black; AL; AL; AL; - ; March; Old Age;
Escambia

WADE, [unreadable]; 93; F; Black; AL; AL; AL; - ; June; Old
Age; Escambia

WADE, [unreadable]; 23; F; Mu; FL; FL; FL; Washing; June;
Dropsy; Escambia

WADE, Irene; 2; F; Mu; FL; FL; FL; - ; June; Dropsy; Escambia

Name; Age; Sex; Race; Born; FABorn; MOBorn;
        Occup; DODeath; Cause Of Death; County

WADE, Agnes; 1; F; Mu; FL; FL; FL; - ; June; Lockjaw;
    Escambia
HELKER, Cerena; 50; F; Black; AL; AL; AL; Cook; March;
    Dropsy; Escambia
BAREFOOT, Walter; 26; M; White; GA; GA; GA; Engineer;
    June; Consumption; Escambia
McHEUGH, P.; 1; M; White; FL; Ireland; AL; - ; April; Lockjaw;
    Escambia
JOHNSON, Henry; 4; M; White; FL; Scotland; AL; - ; April;
    Typhoid Fever; Escambia
ACOSTA, Henry; 1; M; White; FL; AL; AL; - ; Aug; Typhoid
    Fever; Escambia
McALLISTER, E; 1; F; White; FL; FL; AL; - ; Aug; Typhoid
    Fever; Escambia
DeLaRUS,Henry; 28; M; White; FL; FL; FL; - ; Nov; Unknown;
    Escambia
DeLaRUS, Maxwell; 1; M; White; AL; FL; AL; - ; June;
    Unknown; Escambia
FURGERSON, Alex; 1; M; White; FL; NY; GA; - ; March;
    Unknown; Escambia
FURGERSON, [unreadable]; 23; F; White; AL; AL; AL; - ; May;
    Consumption; Escambia
STOKES, B.; 1; F; White; FL; FL; FL; - ; - ; Typhoid Fever;
    Escambia
JOHNSON, [unreadable]; 2; F; Black; AL; AL; AL; - ; June;
    Typhoid Fever; Escambia
GOODMAN, [unreadable]; 4; F; White; AL; AL; AL; - ; May;
    Pneumonia; Escambia
SUNDAY, [unreadable]; 1; M; Mu; FL; FL; AL; - ; June;
    Pneumonia; Escambia
LYMAN, Lewis; 43; M; White; AL; AL; AL; - ; July;
    Consumption; Escambia
TELFAIR, Wm.; 25; M; White; FL; FL; FL; - ; April; Killed by
    Engine; Escambia
JUIESTRA, M. G.; 49; M; White; FL; Spain; FL; - ; Feb; Killed
    by Engine; Escambia
VIRGIL, Robert; 7; M; Black; FL; FL; FL; - ; Oct; Lockjaw;
    Escambia

KING, Anna; 70; F; Black; AL; AL; AL; - ; April; Remittent
Fever; Escambia
HOLLY, C.H.; 65; M; White; GA; GA; GA; - ; July; Cancer;
Escambia
OLIVER, Scott; 22; M; Mu; AL; AL; AL; - ; April; Typhoid
Fever; Escambia
JENKINS, Phoebe; 76; F; Black; AL; AL; AL; - ; July; Scarlet
Fever; Escambia
MILLER, Robert; 40; M; Black; AL; AL; AL; - ; Oct; Pneumonia;
Escambia
DOUGLAS, Mary; 26; F; Black; FL; VA; AL; - ; July;
Consumption; Escambia
JOHNSON, Thos.; 18; M; Black; AL; AL; AL; - ; Nov; Murdered;
Escambia
MITCHELL, Dr.; 75; M; White; VA; VA; VA; - ; Nov; Paralysis;
Escambia
AMOS, C.; 50; F; White; AL; AL; AL; - ; April; Consumption;
Escambia
COOK, Nancy; 25; F; Mu; FL; - ; VA; - ; May; Dropsy; Escambia
MILLER, John; 56; M; White; NY; - ; - ; - ; Jan; Unknown;
Escambia
PERRY, Morgan; 12; M; Black; FL; NC; FL; - ; July; Lightning;
Escambia
McCRAY, Mary; 43; F; Black; FL; NC; FL; - ; Feb; Carbuncle;
Escambia
SHEARS, Phoebe; 42; F; Black; FL; FL; FL; - ; June; White
Swelling; Escambia
LEAKE, Esther; 50; F; White; ENG; ENG; ENG; - ; May;
Paralysis; Escambia
SUARIS, Rebecca; 38; F; White; FL; - ; - ; - ; Jan; Pneumonia;
Escambia
SUARIS, Frank; 1; M; White; FL; - ; ENG; - ; Dec; Pneumonia;
Escambia
TAYLOR, George; 42; M; Black; FL; FL; FL; - ; Sept;
Consumption; Escambia
SCHRODER, Adolph; 28; M; White; LA; AK; GA; Merchant;
Feb; Pneumonia; Escambia

STEVENSON, Aley; 30; F; Black; FL; AL; AL; - ; May;
Unknown; Escambia

SIMS, Clara; 24; F; Black; FL; FL; FL; - ; March; Cholera
Infection; Escambia

TOLIVER, Alfred; 1; M; Black; FL; FL; FL; - ; Mar; Lockjaw;
Escambia

TURNER, Wm. H.; 52; M; White; NY; - ; - ; - ; Oct; Dropsy;
Escambia

VOGEL, Horace; 39; M; Black; AL; - ; - ; - ; June; Dropsy;
Escambia

WILLIAMS, Robt.; 70; M; Black; FL; VA; FL; - ; May; Dropsy;
Escambia

WHITHEAD, Hannah; 22; F; Black; FL; NC; - ; - ; March;
Consumption; Escambia

WRIGHT, Henry; 4; M; White; FL; FL; LA; - ; Mar; - ; Escambia

WHITE, Martha; 39; F; Black; FL; AFRICA; NC; - ; Aug;
Consumption; Escambia

YOUNG, Mary; 30; F; Black; FL; FL; NC; - ; Mar; Chil bed
fever; Escambia

YOUNG, Baby; 1; - ; Black; FL; FL; FL; - ; Mar; Stillborn;
Escambia

THOMPSON, Sallie; 10; F; Black; AL; AL; AL; - ; Jan; Dropsy;
Escambia

ABERCROMBIE, C. A.; 33; M; White; AL; GA; GA; Inspector;
Jan; Pneumonia; Escambia

ABERCROMBIE, J. B.; 28; M; White; AL; GA; GA; Clerk; Dec;
Hematoma; Escambia

ADAMS, J. L.; 3; M; Black; FL; MS; AL; - ; Nov; Scarlet Fever;
Escambia

ALEXANDER, Peter; 36; M; Black; FL; - ; VA; - ; Jan; Dropsy;
Escambia

BECK, C. G.; 21; M; White; FL; GA; GA; Printer; July; Typhoid
Fever; Escambia

BECK, Henry; 19; M; White; FL; GA; GA; Wheelwright; July;
Typhoid Fever; Escambia

BELL, Levi; 40; M; Black; AL; AL; AL; - ; Jan; Old hurt [?];
Escambia

BROWN, Isaac; 60; M; White; VA; VA; VA; - ; Sept; Paralysis;
Escambia
BUTLER, Louisa; 19; F; Black; FL; VA; FL; - ; Feb; Unknown;
Escambia
BUTLER, Mary Ann; 1; F; Black; FL; VA; FL; - ; - ; Unknown;
Escambia
COLLINS, Julius; 1; M; Mu; FL; FL; AL; - ; May; Tetnus;
Escambia
COLLINS, Edmund; 1; M; Mu; FL; FL; AL; - ; Oct; Cold &
Teething; Escambia
CLARKE, Isaac; 1; M; Black; FL; MD; AL; - ; Jan; Lockjaw;
Escambia
CLARKE, Baby; - ; F; Black; FL; MD; AL; - ; Mar; Stillborn;
Escambia
COLLINS, Baby; 1; F; Mu; FL; FL; FL; - ; June; Unknown;
Escambia
COLEMAN, Eliza; 32; F; Black; AL; - ; - ; - ; June; Heart
Disease; Escambia
CLIFFORD, Daisy; 1; F; - ; FL; FL; FL; - ; Nov; Dropsy;
Escambia
COLEMAN, A.; 70; F; White; Ireland; Ireland; Ireland; - ; Oct;
Unknown; Escambia
EDMUND, Frank; 80; M; Black; VA; VA; VA; - ; Oct; Gangreen;
Escambia
GARDENIA, Nick; 80; M; White; FL; Italy; FL; - ; July; Brain
Fever; Escambia
GIVINS, Chas.; 19; M; Black; FL; VA; AL; - ; Dec; Apoplexy;
Escambia
HERNNDEZ, H; 20; M; Mu; FL; FL; FL; Laborer; Jan; Brain
Fever; Escambia
HARRIS, Eady; 1; F; Black; FL; FL; FL; - ; Mar; Unknown;
Escambia
HARRIS, Baby; 1; F; Black; FL; FL; FL; - ; - ; Unknown;
Escambia
HARRIS, Lilly; 1; F; Black; FL; GA; VA; - ; Aug; Teething;
Escambia
KAGE, Randolph; 1; M; White; FL; GA; GA; - ; June; Cholera
Infection; Escambia

20   Name; Age; Sex; Race; Born; FABorn; MOBorn;
        Occup; DODeath; Cause Of Death; County

KING, Julia; 1; F; Black; FL; VA; AL; - ; April; Unknown;
    Escambia
KEMP, Ed; 30; M; Black; AL; AL; AL; - ; July; Consumption;
    Escambia
BALL, Levi; 55; M; Black; GA; - ; - ; - ; June; Cramps; Escambia
McCALLEN, C.; 9; F; Black; AL; SC; AL; - ; Oct; Pneumonia;
    Escambia
MOSLEY, Mary; 84; F; Black; NC; NC; NC; - ; Jan;
    Hemorrhage/lungs; Escambia
BANKS, Stephen; 50; M; Black; FL; FL; FA; - ; Dec;
    Consumption; Escambia
BETHEWSHER, H. A. (?); 1; M; Black; FL; MI; AL; - ; April; - ;
    Escambia
AINSWORTH, G [--]; 1; M; White; FL; AL; FL; - ; April;
    Lockjaw; Escambia
MITCHELL, A.; 10; M; Black; FL; AL; SC; - ; Jan; Drowned;
    Escambia
MITCHELL, Col; 7; M; Black; FL; AL; SC; - ; Jan; Drowned;
    Escambia
UNION, Aaron; 48; M; Black; AL; AL; SC; Laborer; Jan;
    Malarial Fever; Escambia
VAUGHN, Bell; 15; F; White; FL; AL; FL; - ; May; Malarial
    Fever; Escambia
JACKSON, F.; 25; F; Black; FL; VA; VA; - ; Feb; Dropsy;
    Escambia
KING, F. M. G.; 54; M; White; TN; AL; FL; Carpenter; May;
    Dropsy; Escambia
KING, David; 31; M; White; TN; Al; FL; Farmer; Jan;
    Consumption; Escambia
YOUNG, Willie; 5; M; Black; FL; MD; FL; - ; June; Bilious
    Fever; Escambia
JONES, Elsie; 30; F; Black; SC; SC; SC; - ; June; Poisoned;
    Escambia
WILLIAM, Adner; 4; M; Black; FL; AL; GA; - ; Sept; Fever;
    Escambia
DAWSON, M.; 13; F; Black; FL; GA; AL; - ; Feb; Consumption;
    Escambia
S[----]H, Lena; 12; F; Black; FL; AL; FL; - ; Jan; Fever; Escambia

WHITE, Wyatt; 17; M; Black; FL; FL; AL; Brakeman; June;
Killed on RR; Escambia

RICHARDSON, P.; 1; M; Black; FL; VA; MD; - ; Jan; Debility;
Escambia

GRICE, Lucinda; 35; F; Black; Al; - ; AL; - ; Dec; Consumption;
Escambia

GOHLSLEN, Winnie; - ; F; Black; FL; - ; AL; - ; May; Stillborn;
Escambia

BARLOW, Sarah; 15; F; Black; AL; - ; SC; - ; Jan; Dropsy;
Escambia

ADAMS, Nathan; 45; M; Black; AL; AL; AL; Carpenter; June;
Dropsy; Escambia

SAMUEL, Dan'l.; 80; M; Black; GA; VA; VA; Laborer; Dec;
Gravel; Escambia

ENTERKIN, Jas.; 23; M; White; FL; FL; FL; Laborer; Nov;
Pneumonia; Escambia

BUSBY, Denis; 1; M; White; AL; AL; AL; - ; Sept; Typhoid
Fever; Escambia

TAYLOR, I. C.; 48; M; White; FL; - ; FL; Laborer; April;
Consumption; Escambia

DAVIS, John; - ; M; White; FLA; - ; - ; - ; April; Stillborn;
Escambia

RICHARDSON, M.; 15; F; White; AL; - ; GA; - ; Feb;
Hemorrhage; Escambia

SALTER, Solomon; 1; M; White; FL; - ; - ; - ; - ; Unknown;
Escambia

COLE, Mary Ann; 4; F; Black; FL; AL; LA; - ; Jan; Malarial
Fever; Escambia

SHEPARD, Daniel; 76; M; White; GA; - ; - ; Farmer; June;
Unknown; Escambia

BAILEY, Martha; 33; F; White; AL; - ; - ; - ; July; Rheumatism;
Escambia

BRIT, Thomas; 6; M; Black; FL; AL; AL; - ; March; Croup;
Escambia

LANELL, Clara; 5; F; White; AL; - ; - ; - ; Oct; Putrid sore throat;
Escambia

LANELL, M. L.; 69; M; White; NH; - ; - ; Farmer; Mar; Bright's
Disease; Escambia

Name; Age; Sex; Race; Born; FABorn; MOBorn;
         Occup; DODeath; Cause Of Death; County

TATE, M. F.; 3; F; White; FL; - ; - ; - ; Feb; Congestion Brain;
    Escambia
HIGH, L. T.; 45; M; White; MS; - ; - ; Saw Filer; Dec;
    Menningitis; Escambia
TAPIOLA, Peter; 31; M; White; FL; - ; - ; - ; Dec; Insane;
    Escambia
WOOD, Margaret; 49; F; Black; AL; - ; - ; - ; Aug; Dropsy;
    Escambia
GRICE, Joseph; 50; W; Black; AL; - ; - ; - ; April; Dropsy;
    Escambia
HASTINGS, Laura; 28; F; White; FL; KY; AL; - ; Oct; Fever;
    Escambia
RANDOLPH, H.; 1; M; White; Al; SC; SC; - ; Feb; Spasms;
    Escambia
PRICE, B. F.; 48; M; White; TN; - ; - ; - ; July; Heart Disease;
    Escambia
WILLIAMS, Mrs. Robt; - ; F; White; FL; - ; - ; - ; Sept; Child
    Birth; Escambia
EDDINS, Rebecca; 72; F; White; AL; - ; - ; - ; May; Debility;
    Escambia
BLACKWELL, Noah; 45; M; White; AL; - ; - ; - ; May;
    Pneumonia; Escambia
GODFREY, Herbert; 3; M; White; FL; - ; - ; - ; May; Typhoid
    Fever; Escambia
McCURDY, Alonzo; 3; M; White; FL; - ; - ; - ; June; Dropsy;
    Escambia
McCURDY, Flora; 1; F; White; FL; - ; - ; - ; Aug; Scarlet Fever;
    Escambia
JACKSON, Abe; 25; M; Black; AL; AL; - ; - ; May; Killed on
    RR; Escambia
LEWIS, Susan; 23; F; White; AL; - ; - ; - ; April; Mal. Fever;
    Escambia
McCULLUCH, A; 1; M; Black; FL; - ; - ; - ; May; Mal. Fever;
    Escambia
PENNEL, Mary; 45; F; White; FL; - ; - ; - ; June; Change of life;
    Escambia
BOORK, John; 1; M; White; FL; FL; AL; - ; July; Tumor;
    Escambia

ECKTEBERGER, John; 60; M; White; Ger; - ; - ; Seaman; Oct;
Remittent Fever; Franklin

BROWN, Emma; 6; F; Black; FL; FL; FL; - ; Oct; Unknown;
Franklin

HAND, Bryant; 1; M; Black; FL; FL; FL; - ; Nov; Unknown;
Franklin

RIDLER, Georgie; 40; F; Black; GA; - ; - ; - ; Aug; Unknown;
Franklin

BUSH, Charity; 56; F; Black; GA; - ; - ; - ; May; Unknown;
Franklin

PRICE, Jensey; 50; F; Black; GA; - ; - ; - ; May; Unknown;
Franklin

LEGREE, Wm. T.; 1; M; White; FL; FL; FL; - ; May; Unknown;
Franklin

HILL, R. L.; 1; M; White; FL; FL; FL; - ; May; Remittent Fever;
Franklin

WILLSON, Clara; 70; F; Black; SC; - ; - ; - ; May; Unknown;
Franklin

THOMPSON, Lizzie; 40; F; Black; FL; - ; - ; - ; May; Thorasic
A[?]; Franklin

WELCH, Margaret; 27; F; White; FL; - ; - ; - ; April; Unknown;
Franklin

LUATZ, Henry; 26; M; White; GER; - ; - ; - ; April; Drowned;
Franklin

COLANELL, E. D.; 23; M; Black; FL; - ; - ; - ; Mar; Drowned;
Franklin

NAVIN, Robert; 21; M; Black; FL; - ; - ; - ; Mar; Drowned;
Franklin

WELCH, Infant; 1; M; White; FL; FL; FL; - ; Mar; Unknown;
Franklin

WELCH, Infant; 1; M; White; FL; FL; FL; - ; Mar; Unknown;
Franklin

LEGREE, Jossey; 1; M; White; FL; FL; FL; - ; Mar; Congestion
Brain; Franklin

CLARK, Mrs. J. L.; 40; F; White; ME; - ; - ; - ; Mar; Congestive
fever; Franklin

MEADLY, Jas.; 56; M; White; Ireland; - ; - ; - ; Mar; Unknown;
Franklin

24   Name; Age; Sex; Race; Born; FABorn; MOBorn;
            Occup; DODeath; Cause Of Death; County

SIMMONS, Jas.; 24; M; Black; FL; - ; - ; - ; Feb; Drowned;
    Franklin
YON, Isaac; 43; M; White; GA; - ; - ; - ; Feb; Diarrhea; Franklin
DALY, Hatie; 18; F; White; Canada; - ; - ; - ; July; Cerebitis;
    Franklin
MADDOX, Wm.; 1; M; White; FL; FL; FL; - ; June; Unknown;
    Franklin
STEPHENS, Wm.; 1; M; White; FL; FL; FL; - ; July; Unknown;
    Franklin
GLANT, Mrs.; 60; F; White; States; - ; - ; - ; July;
    Cancer/stomach; Franklin
COOK, Maggill; 12; F; Black; FL; FL; FL; - ; Aug; Unknown;
    Franklin
WITHERSPOON, Mucky; 20; M; White; FL; FL; Fl; - ; Aug;
    Congestion Brain; Franklin
ASHER, Geo.; 50; M; White; Eng; - ; - ; - ; Aug; Apoplexy;
    Franklin
HUMPHRIES, S.C.; 45; F; White; Eng; - ; - ; - ; Aug; Unknown;
    Franklin
CAMPBELL, Gaston; 2; M; White; FL; - ; - ; - ; Aug; Congestion
    Brain; Franklin
MESSINA, Magella; 7; F; White; FL; Italy; Portugal; - ; Aug;
    Congestion Brain; Franklin
SELVIA, Antonie; 24; M; Black; GA; - ; - ; - ; Sept; Unknown;
    Franklin
SHARITT, Bose; 4; M; White; FL; NY; FL; - ; Sept; Unknown;
    Franklin
WENG, Robt.; 21; M; White; FL; - ; FL; - ; Jan; Unknown;
    Franklin
CULLEN, Sarah; 37; F; White; FL; - ; FL; - ; Jan; Diarrhea;
    Franklin
CURTIS, Lonza; 7; M; Black; FL; SC; SC; - ; July; Abcess in
    head; Gadsden
FULGER, -------- ; 1; F; Black; FL; FL; FL; - ; May; Unknown;
    Gadsden
SHELBY, Willie; 1; M; Black; FL; FL; FL; - ; Oct; Unknown;
    Gadsden

ALDERMAN, Geo.; 22; M; White; FL; FL; FL; Farmer; Oct;
Typhoid Fever; Gadsden

OWENS,----- ; - ; - ; - ; - ; - ; - ; - ; - ; Stillborn; Gadsden

ROBINSON, Thos. H.; 18; M; White; FL; - ; - ; - ; - ; Typhoid
Fever; Gadsden

WALSH, Florence; 13; F; White; FL; FL; FL; - ; - ; Unknown;
Gadsden

SCOTT, G. W. ; 2; M; White; FL; GA; FL; - ; June; Brain Fever;
Gadsden

SCOTT, Leonidus; 56; M; White; FL; - ; GA; Dentist; Nov; Heart
Disease; Gadsden

TRULOCK, G. L.; 5; M; White; FL; GA; GA; - ; Sept; Bilious
Fever; Gadsden

TRULOCK, Anna; 1; F; White; FL; GA; GA; - ; Sept; Unknown;
Gadsden

LAMBERT, O. J.; 15; M; White; FL; FL; FL; - ; Sept; Dropsy;
Gadsden

DISMMUKES, Jns.; 3; M; - ; FL; TN; TN; - ; Mar; Stomach
Cong.; Gadsden

HARRIS, M. D. G.; - ; F; - ; - ; - ; - ; - ; - ; Unknown; Gadsden

WILSON, E. Maria; 37; F; - ; FL; SC; - ; - ; May; Unknown;
Gadsden

WASHINGTON, Geo; 50; M; Black; FL; - ; - ; - ; Jan;
Pneumonia; Gadsden

STEARN, Emmet; 2; M; White; FL; ME; FL; - ; Nov;
Inflam/stomach; Gadsden

MAY, Fred; 4; M; White; FL; FL; FL; - ; Nov;
Congestion/bowels; Gadsden

LOVE, M. J.; 50; F; White; FL; - ; - ; - ; - ; Heart Disease;
Gadsden

WASHINGTON, Dan; 54; M; Black; - ; - ; - ; - ; - ; Unknown;
Gadsden

BALDWIN, Cleavland; 1; M; Black; FL; FL; FL; - ; Jan;
Overlaid; Gadsden

FITZGERALD, Edgar; 5; M; Black; FL; FL; FL; - ; Nov; Fever;
Gadsden

EPPES, Henrietta; 13; F; Black; FL; FL; FL; - ; Nov; Spinal;
Gadsden

Name; Age; Sex; Race; Born; FABorn; MOBorn;
          Occup; DODeath; Cause Of Death; County

COOPER, Eliza; 21; F; Black; FL; SC; SC; Laborer; May;
     Unknown; Gadsden
BRAXTON, Corbin; 70; M; Black; VA; - ; - ; Farmer; Sept; Heart
     Disease; Gadsden
GIBSON, Margaret; 21; F; Black; FL; FL; NC; - ; Oct; Child Bed;
     Gadsden
COLLIER, Betsy; 50; F; Black; - ; - ; - ; - ; June; Inflammation;
     Gadsden
CHANDLER, Rosetta; 80; F; Black; SC; SC; SC; - ; Mar;
     Paralysis; Gadsden
McNEAL, H. W.; 1; M; Black; FL; - ; FL; - ; Nov; Hives;
     Gadsden
SMITH, S. C.; 9; F; White; FL; FL; FL; - ; Sept; Bilious Fever;
     Gadsden
BANKS, Nellie; 1; F; Black; FL; FL; FL; - ; Feb; Cholera
     Infection; Gadsden
SIMMONS, Tom; 70; M; Black; SC; SC; SC; Farmer; May; Gen.
     Debility; Gadsden
HOLMES, Sarah; 83; F; Black; GA; SC; SC; - ; Nov; Burnt;
     Gadsden
RICHARDSON, Rowanna; 2; F; Black; GA; SC; SC; - ; Nov;
     Dysentery; Gadsden
GILCHRIST, Alex; 31; M; White; FL; NC; NC; Farmer; Aug; - ;
     Gadsden
CRISWELL, Geo.; 27; M; White; SC; SC; SC; Railroad; Dec;
     Typhoid Fever; Gadsden
MARTIN, M.; 61; M; Black; Ireland; Ireland; Ireland; - ; Aug;
     Congestion; Gadsden
WALKER, Chas.; 24; M; Black; FL; FL; FL; Laborer; Feb;
     Typhoid Fever; Gadsden
HAGGET, Lafaette; 72; M; Black; FL; GA; GA; Preacher; Dec;
     Dropsy; Gadsden
ATWATER, Minah; 40; F; Black; FL; NC; NC; Housewife; Mar;
     Unknown; Gadsden
SILAS, Nicy; 49; F; White; FL; FL; FL; Housewife; Oct;
     Unknown; Gadsden
PEACOCK, Florence; 17; F; White; FL; FL; FL; Housewife; Feb;
     Pulmonary; Gadsden

McALPIN, A. L.; 5; M; White; FL; FL; FL; Housewife; Sept; Pneumonia; Gadsden

RAMSEY, E. J.; 1; F; White; FL; KY; TN; - ; Nov; Pneumonia; Gadsden

HARE, D. W.; 30; M; White; FL; NC; FL; Farmer; Dec; Bright's Disease; Gadsden

SABERS, Jessie; 11; M; White; FL; FL; FL; - ; Feb; Congestion; Gadsden

GOODSON, Elona; 2; F; White; Fl; GA; FL; - ; Sept; Bright's Disease; Gadsden

HARRISON, Sylvia; 50; F; Black; FL; SC; SC; - ; June; Unknown; Gadsden

GEE, Liza; 10; F; Black; FL; FL; FL; - ; Aug; Unknown; Gadsden

GEE, David; 4; M; White; FL; FL; FL; - ; July; Congestion; Gadsden

ROBINSON, Nancy; 80; F; Black; FL; - ; - ; - ; April; Fell dead; Gadsden

NELSON, Felson J.; 1; M; Black; FL; GA; GA; - ; April; Unknown; Gadsden

SHAN, M. E.; 56; F; White; FL; - ; - ; - ; Nov; Consumption; Gadsden

FLOYD, Geo. W.; 80; M; White; - ; - ; - ; - ; Sept; Unknown; Gadsden

JUDESON, Amy; 35; F; Black; FL; FL; FL; Painter; Sept; Consumption; Gadsden

JACKSON, Mary; 1; F; Black; FL; FL; FL; - ; - ; Unknown; Gadsden

SAPP, Abram; 4; M; Black; FL; FL; FL; - ; - ; Burned; Gadsden

STATEMAN, Lug; 3; F; Black; FL; FL; FL; - ; - ; Worms; Gadsden

LOVE, Ann; 78; F; White; NC; Scotland; NC; - ; Oct; Unknown; Gadsden

KILBY, Rosabell; 20; F; Black; FL; FL; FL; - ; Oct; Consumption; Gadsden

SHIVERS, Jonas; 35; M; Black; FL; - ; - ; Farmer; May; Dropsy; Gadsden

WILLIAMS, Sr., Robt.; 79; M; Black; - ; - ; - ; Farmer; Jan; Old Age; Gadsden

　　　　Name; Age; Sex; Race; Born; FABorn; MOBorn;
　　　　Occup; DODeath; Cause Of Death; County

HOWARD, Dennis; 11; M; Black; FL; - ; FL; - ; Mar; Killed by
　　Polecat; Gadsden
HALL, Guilford; 54; M; Black; NC; - ; - ; Farmer; Aug;
　　Unknown; Gadsden
NIXON, James; 14; M; Black; FL; FL; FL; - ; March; Dropsy;
　　Gadsden
WILLIAMS, Florence; 12; F; Black; FL; FL; FL; - ; Oct;
　　Unknown; Gadsden
CLEM, Hilliard; 48; M; Black; FL; - ; - ; Farmer; Aug;
　　Consumption; Gadsden
SMITH, R. L.; 4; M; Black; FL; FL; FL; - ; Sept; Worms;
　　Gadsden
HARVEY, Allen; 1; M; Black; FL; FL; FL; - ; March; Unknown;
　　Gadsden
MORGAN, Nancy; 10; F; Black; FL; FL; FL; - ; Sept; Unknown;
　　Gadsden
FILLYACE, Amy; 100; F; Black; NC; - ; - ; - ; Jan; Old Age;
　　Gadsden
THOMAS, Patten; 23; F; Black; FL; GA; SC; - ; June; Unknown;
　　Gadsden
FERGERSON, Julia; 14; F; Black; FL; FL; FL; Laborer; May;
　　Unknown; Gadsden
WELLS, -------- ; 1; F; Black; FL; NC; FL; - ; Aug; Fever;
　　Gadsden
PRICHARD, Mollie; 17; F; White; FL; GA; GA; - ; Mar; Burning;
　　Gadsden
MADNY, J.; 1; M; Black; FL; FL; FL; - ; Oct; Hives; Gadsden
MADNY, ----- ; 1; M; Black; FL; FL; FL; - ; July; Unknown;
　　Gadsden
BETSIC, --- ; - ; - ; Black; FL; FL; FL; - ; - ; Stillborn; Gadsden
HOUSE, -------- ; - ; - ; Black; FL; FL; FL; - ; July; Stillborn;
　　Gadsden
COWARD, R.; 1; F; Black; - ; - ; - ; - ; Jan; Fever; Gadsden
HOON, S.; 55; M; Black; VA; - ; - ; Laborer; Sept; Pneumonia;
　　Gadsden
DIXON, H.; 38; F; Black; FL; NC; NC; Laborer; June; Liver
　　Disease; Gadsden

WILLIAMS, -------- ; 1; F; White; FL; GA; GA; - ; Feb; Fever;
Gadsden

OWENS, C. C.; 75; F; White; FL; GA; GA; Housewife; June;
General A[?]; Gadsden

BRADWELL, ---------- ; 1; F; Black; FL; SC; FL; - ; Dec;
Pneumonia; Gadsden

RUDD, W. R.; 9; M; White; FL; FL; FL; - ; May; Inflam/bowels;
Gadsden

BAINY, G.; 2; M; Black; FL; FL; FL; - ; May; Dysentery;
Gadsden

JONES, E.; 4; F; Black; FL; GA; FL; - ; May; Pneumonia;
Gadsden

BRADWELL, ---------- ; 1; F; Black; FL; SC; SC; - ; Sept;
Unknown; Gadsden

WOODBERRY, D.; 80; M; Black; FL; - ; - ; - ; Dec; Old Age;
Gadsden

RUDD, -------- ; 1; M; White; FL; FL; FL; - ; Nov; Unknown;
Gadsden

HAYGOOD, -------- ; 1; M; Black; FL; SC; SC; - ; Aug;
Unknown; Gadsden

BLOUNT, H.; 2; M; White; FL; FL; FL; - ; Aug; Bilious Fever;
Gadsden

McCATHUM, H.; 90; F; White; NC; NC; NC; Housewife; June;
Rheumatism; Gadsden

PARAMOR, E. A.; 50; F; White; SC; SC; SC; Housewife; March;
Pneumonia; Gadsden

THARP, S.; 15; F; White; FL; GA; GA; - ; April; Unknown;
Gadsden

THARP, B.; 8; F; White; FL; GA; GA; - ; May; Dropsy; Gadsden

EVANS, Steven; 56; M; Black; SC; SC; SC; Farmer; Feb;
Consumption; Gadsden

BELL, Eliza; 40; F; Black; FL; - ; - ; - ; Mar; Pneumonia; Gadsden

MILLER, William; 3; M; Mu; FL; SC; FL; - ; Feb; Fever;
Gadsden

KENAN, Sam; 11; M; Black; FL; NC; NC; - ; Nov; Brain Fever;
Gadsden

MILLER, Ed; 2; M; Mu; FL; SC; FL; - ; June; Yellow Thrush;
Gadsden

Name; Age; Sex; Race; Born; FABorn; MOBorn;
Occup; DODeath; Cause Of Death; County

WESTON, Allen; 6; M; Black; FL; FL; FL; - ; Jan; Brain Fever;
Gadsden
WESTON, Jane; 1; M; Black; FL; FL; FL; - ; Mar; Pneumonia;
Gadsden
WILLIAMS, Lettie; 1; F; Black; FL; SC; SC; - ; Aug; Bilious
Fever; Gadsden
GREGORY, Minerva; 5; F; Black; FL; GA; VA; - ; Feb;
Pneumonia; Gadsden
GREGORY, Catie; 1; F; Black; FL; GA; VA; - ; Oct; Unknown;
Gadsden
SIMS, Catie; 60; F; Black; - ; - ; - ; - ; Jan; Dropsy; Gadsden
ROBINSON, Robt.; 85; M; Black; VA; VA; VA; - ; Mar;
Unknown; Gadsden
WILLIAMS, May; 84; M; Black; - ; - ; - ; Farmer; - ; Old Age;
Gadsden
ROBINSON, Gennie; 2; M; Black; FL; - ; - ; - ; Unknown;
Gadsden
ROBINSON, Jeff; 25; M; Black; GA; GA; GA; - ; Aug;
Rheumatism; Gadsden
DABNER, Geo.; 2; M; Black; FL; SC; FL; - ; July; Pneumonia;
Gadsden
HUDNALL, Mac; 64; M; Black; SC; - ; - ; - ; - ; Unknown;
Gadsden
CANTY, Catherine; 40; F; White; FL; SC; SC; - ; Jan; Bronchitis;
Gadsden
CANTY, L. M.; 15; F; White; SC; SC; FL; - ; April; Burned;
Gadsden
JACKSON, Jesse E.; 5; M; Black; FL; GA; GA; - ; Feb;
Convulsions; Gadsden
WATSON, Hattie; 7; F; White; FL; FL; GA; - ; June; Died from
fall; Gadsden
STOPHARD (?), Fannie; 60; - ; - ; SC; SC; GA; - ; June;
Dysentery; Gadsden
ROBINSON, M. L.; 1; - ; - ; FL; FL; FL; - ; Jan; Unknown;
Gadsden
BROWNING, Jas.; 3; - ; - ; FL; - ; AL; - ; May; Burned; Gadsden
McCALL, A. B.; 3; M; White; FL; GA; GA; - ; Oct; Diptheria;
Hamilton

SMITH, M. E.; 20; F; White; GA; GA; GA; - ; Nov; [unreadable];
Hamilton

ROGERS, Wm.; 6; M; White; FL; GA; GA; - ; Sept; Congestion
Brain; Hamilton

ROGERS, E.; 3; F; White; FL; GA; GA; - ; Sept; Congestion
Brain; Hamilton

BREMAN, J. ; 20; F; White; FL; GA; GA; Housewife; Dec;
Malarial Fever; Hamiton

SHELL, Jessy; 35; M; Black; SC; SC; SC; Farmer; Jan;
Consumption; Hamilton

PASTELL, P. A.; 28; M; Black; GA; BA; GA; Farmer; March;
Pneumonia; Hamilton

EDWARDS, Richard; 50; M; Black; GA; GA; GA; Farmer ;
March; Pneumonia; Hamilton

HAYWARD, James; 40; M; Black; SC; SC; SC; Farmer; March;
Pneumonia; Hamilton

JOHNS, C. I.; 4; M; White; FL; GA; GA; - ; May; [?] Bowels;
Hamilton

BELL, M. H.; 51; F; White; FL; NC; GA; - ; July; [unreadable];
Hamilton

DEMPSEY, Margaret; 70; F; White; SC; SC; SC; Housewife;
Sept; Dropsy; Hamilton

BUSH, C. C.; 12; M; White; FL; - ; GA; Farmer; July; Brain
Fever; Hamilton

BROWN, Sarah; 45; F; White; GA; GA; GA; Housewife; - ;
Consumption; Hamilton

Dees, A.; 17; F; White; FL; FL; FL; - ; - ; Child Birth; Hamilton

[unreadable], Lili; 5; F; White; FL; FL; FL; - ; Jan; Smith;
Hamilton

BROWN, H. A.; 4; F; White; FL; FL; FL; - ; Oct.; Diptheria;
Hamilton

MED [unreadable], Pastell; 4; M; Black; FL; AL; SC; - ; - ; - ;
Hamilton

M [unreadable], M.A.; 52; F; White; GA; GA; GA; Housewife;
July; Congestion; Hamilton

H [unreadable], B.; 5; M; White; FL; FL; FL; - ; Oct; Brain Fever;
Hamilton

RATLIFF, A. G.; 34; M; White; GA; GA; GA; Farmer; Dec; - ;
Hamilton

INGRAM, E M.; 42; M; White; FL; GA; FL; - ; May; Pneumonia;
Hamilton

HENDERSON, D. M.; 4; M; White; GA; GA; GA; - ; - ;
Diptheria; Hamilton

ARNOLD, Caroline; 18; F; White; GA; GA; GA; Housewife; Feb;
Cirrhosis liver; Hamilton

ARNOLD, Nellie; 1; F; White; FL; GL; GA; - ; April; Cholera
Infection; Hamilton

THOMAS, William; 2; M; White; FL; GA; FL; - ; April; Typhoid
Fever; Hamilton

WILLIAMS, H. P.; 1; M; White; FL; FL; FL; - ; June; - ;
Hamilton

DENE [unreadable], H.; 59; F; Black; GA; GA; GA; Washing;
May; Bilious Fever; Hamilton

LAND, Andrew; 20; M; White; GA; GA; GA; Farmer; Dec;
Consumption ; Hamilton

WARD, Jane; 62; F; White; TN; NC; NC; Housewife; April;
Pneumonia; Hamilton

JOHNSON, Ira; 19; M; White; FL; GA; GA; Farmer; Sept;
Unknown; Hamilton

BRYAN, Mary C.; 35; F; White; FL; SC; FL; Housewife; June;
Unknown; Hamilton

REGISTER, Evie; 1; F; White; FL; FL; FL; - ; June;
Inflam/bowels; Hamilton

SMITH, C. E.; 63; F; White; SC; Ger; SC; Housewife; Mar;
Inflam/bowels; Hamilton

SMITH, C. W.; 1; M; White; FL; GA; GA; - ; Feb; Unknown;
Hamilton

STEPHENS, William; 14; M; White; FL; FL; GA; Farmer; Oct;
Typhoid Fever; Hamilton

BAKER, Lucy; 1; F; Black; FL; GA; GA; - ; July; Bleeding;
Hamilton

MOSES, G.; 3; M; Black; FL; FL; FL; - ; June; Bilious Fever;
Hamilton

SIMMONS, Katie; 3; F; White; FL; GA; GA; - ; Aug;
Inflam/bowels; Hamilton

SIMMONS, R. H.; 1; M; White; FL; GA; GA; - ; Mar;
Inflam/bowels; Hamilton

McDANIEL, Jno.; 66; M; White; NC; NC; NC; Farmer; July;
Cirrhosis liver; Hamilton

MATHIS, Sarah; 15; F; Black; SC; SC; SC; Farmer; April;
Malarial Fever; Hamilton

MOSES, James; 65; M; Black; GA; GA; GA; Farmer; Oct;
Inflam/bowels; Hamilton

TUTEN, Julia; 1; F; White; FL; FL; FL; - ; July; Malarial Fever;
Hamilton

RICE, Wm. G.; 10; M; White; FL; SC; GA; - ; May; Dysentery;
Hamilton

RICE, Rosa G.; 12; F; White; FL; SC; GA; - ; - ; Dysentery;
Hamilton

HALL, A. L.; 63; F; White; FL; GA; GA; Housewife; May;
Unknown; Hamilton

MOSES, Gus; 65; F; Black; SC; SC; SC; - ; June; Dropsy;
Hamilton

JOHNS, W. R.; 55; M; MW; FL; GA; GA; Farmer; Sept; Bilious
Fever; Hamilton

RAULERSON, Hattie; 9; F; White; FL; GA; FL; - ; Aug;
Congestion; Hamilton

HUNTER, ------ R.; 16; F; White; FL; GA; FL; - ; Oct; Unknown;
Hamilton

HUNTER, William; 3; M; White; FL; FL; FL; - ; Oct; Unknown;
Hamilton

WILLIAMS, E. S.; 45; M; White; GA; GA; GA; Farmer; June;
Unknown; Hamilton

[unreadable], W. R.; 40; M; White; GA; GA; GA; Farmer; Aug;
Dropsy; Hamilton

WILKINS, Wm.; 20; M; Black; FL; FL; FL; Laborer; Sept;
Unknown; Hamilton

JOHNSON, A. H.; 3; M; Black; FL; Nassau; FL; - ; June; Malarial
Fever; Hernando

MILLEN, C.; 10; M; White; KY; KY; KY; - ; Nov; Brain Fever;
Hernando

MILLEN, B.; 14; M; White; KY; KY; KY; - ; Nov; Unknown;
Hernando

Name; Age; Sex; Race; Born; FABorn; MOBorn;
          Occup; DODeath; Cause Of Death; County

BROWN, Green; 40; M; White; GA; GA; GA; - ; Feb; Erysipelas;
    Hernando
JORDAN, H.; 50; M; White; FL; GA; GA; - ; Oct; Malarial Fever;
    Hernando
SNIDER, G.; 30; M; White; GA; GA; GA; - ; Sept; Malarial
    Fever; Hernando
GIDDENS, D.; 45; M; White; GA; GA; GA; - ; Feb; Bilious
    Fever; Hernando
FENDON, D.; 65; M; White; NJ; NJ; NJ; - ; April; Bilious Fever;
    Hernando
HALL, I.; 4; F; White; FL; FL; FL; - ; Mar; Cancer; Hernando
GREEN, W. W.; 17; M; White; TN; MO; TX; - ; Sept; Scrofila(?);
    Hernando
TUCKER, Jim; 4; M; White; FL; FL; FL; - ; Jan; Bilious Fever;
    Hernando
GOMAS, Wm. A.; 1; M; White; FL; FL; FL; - ; Aug; Bilious
    Fever; Hernando
HAY, William; 5; M; White; FL; FL; FL; - ; Mar; Chills & Fever;
    Hernando
HOPKINS, C. W.; 35; M; White; GA; GA; GA; - ; Mar; Fever;
    Hernando
BROWN, Jas. O.; 58; M; White; Al; NY; AL; - ; Aug;
    Rheumatism; Hernando
WILLIAMS, Ross; 23; M; Black; GA; GA; GA; - ; Aug;
    Consumption; Hernando
CLARK, Mary; 48; F; White; FL; FL; FL; - ; May; Dysentery;
    Hernando
ROBERTS, Worth; 1; M; White; FL; FL; FL; - ; Jan; Typhoid
    Fever; Hernando
BAKER, Sami; 3; M; White; FL; FL; FL; - ; Sept; Malarial Fever;
    Hernando
BAKER, Arthur; 1; M; White; FL; FL; FL; - ; Feb; Malarial
    Fever; Hernando
SPRING, Mabel M..; 5; F; White; AL; AL; AL; - ; Oct;
    Congestion Brain; Hernando
GAFFNEY, Sallie C.; 15; F; White; GA; Ireland; GA; - ; Dec;
    Pneumonia; Hernando

DAMPIER, Henrietta; 28; F; White; FL; - ; - ; - ; July; Unknown;
Hernando
FENNELL, Bryant; 25; M; White; GA; - ; - ; - ; July; Lightning;
Hernando
FENNELL, Julia; 25; F; White; GA; - ; - ; - ; July; Lightning;
Hernando
DEWEY, John T.; 21; M; White; VA; VA; VA; - ; June;
Congestion Brain; Hernando
TRYON, Marvin; 84; M; White; VA; SC; VA; - ; Oct; Congestive
chill; Hernando
HODGE, Thos.; 74; M; White; GA; - ; - ; Farmer; June; Heart
Disease; Hernando
MORGAN, Ella; 17; M; White; - ; - ; - ; - ; Oct; Sp. Menningitis;
Hernando
MANN, Ralph; 5; M; White; - ; - ; - ; - ; May; Congestion;
Hernando
MORTON, ------- ; 26; F; White; - ; - ; - ; - ; Nov; Pneumonia;
Hernando
KROUSE, Wm; 20; F; White; - ; - ; - ; - ; Nov; Pneumonia;
Hernando
KROUSE, Virginia; 26; F; White; - ; - ; - ; - ; Feb; Laryngitis;
Hernando
C[unreadable], Lucy; 60; M; White; - ; - ; - ; - ; Aug;
Consumption; Hernando
McCANDLISH, Wm.; 54; W; White; NY; Scotland; Scotland;
Citrus; Nov; Typhoid Fever; Hillsboro.
NELSON, Mary L.; 58; F; White; TN; NC; NC; - ; Oct; Heart
Disease; Hillsboro.
MORRIS, Nellie; 31; F; White; England; - ; - ; Teacher; Oct;
Dysentery; Hillsboro.
WINGATE, Jonathan; 1; M; White; FL; AL; FL; - ; Sept;
Dysentery; Hillsboro.
McCALL, Mrs. H. A.; 37; F; White; GA; GA; GA; - ; April;
Consumption; Hillsboro.
STILLMAN, Perry; 21; M; White; KS; - ; - ; Teamster; Sept;
Typhoid Fever; Hillsboro.
FERRIS, Henry; 73; M; White; NY; - ; - ; Seaman; Nov; Gen.
Decline Age; Hillsboro.

Name; Age; Sex; Race; Born; FABorn; MOBorn;
         Occup; DODeath; Cause Of Death; County

ERWIN, Hattie; 1; F; Black; FL; PA; FL; - ; Aug; Brain Fever;
   Hillsboro.
BROWN, Wm. Henry; 17; M; Black; FL; PA; FL; - ; May;
   Drowning; Hillsboro.
BUTLER, Phillis; 50; F; Black; GA; - ; - ; Washing; Aug;
   Diarrhea; Hillsboro.
LARRY, Amy; 1; F; Black; FL; FL; FL; - ; July; Convulsions;
   Hillsboro.
BOURQUARDEZ, Constance; 60; M; White; France; France;
   France; Carpenter; Sept; Typhoid Fever; Hillsboro.
MANDREE, James; 34; M; White; - ; - ; - ; Carpenter; Sept;
   Typhoid Fever; Hillsboro.
MOORE, Alice; 36; F; White; FL; FL; FL; - ; July; Typhoid
   Fever; Hillsboro.
BOURQUARDEZ, Louisa; 18; F; White; FL; FL; FL; - ; Sept;
   Typhoid Fever; Hillsboro.
MAD[--]E,---- ; 4; M; White; FL; FL; FL; - ; Aug; Typhoid Fever;
   Hillsboro.
DAVIS, Alice U.; 1; F; Black; FL; FL; Bahamas; - ; Feb; Cold &
   Fever; Hillsboro.
STEPHENS, Mary; 30; F; Black; Bahamas; Bahamas; Bahamas; -
   ; Feb; Dropsy; Hillsboro.
WASHINGTON, Charlotte; 23; F; Mu; FL; - ; FL; Housewife;
   May; Consumption; Hillsboro.
O'NEIL, Elisabeth; 7; F; Black; FL; GA; FL; - ; Aug; Malarial
   Fever; Hillsboro.
DePEW, Infant; 1; F; White; FL; IN; VA; - ; Dec; St. Anthony's
   Fire; Hillsboro.
CLAY, Selane; 10; F; Black; FL; FL; FL; - ; Sept; Malarial Fever;
   Hillsboro.
A[unreadable], Henry; 1; M; Black; FL; GA; FL; - ; April;
   Pneumonia; Hillsboro.
ANDERSON, JR, T. J.; 1; M; Black; FL; SC; SC; - ; Sept;
   Dysentery; Hillsboro.
SALTER, Clyde; 1; M; Black; FL; NC; FL; - ; Aug; Congestive
   chill; Hillsboro.
MINICH, Jimme A.; 1; M; White; FL; PA; PA; - ; Oct; White
   Swelling; Hillsboro.

SMITH, Isaac; 56; M; Black; FL; - ; - ; Laborer; - ; Unknown; Hillsboro.

RANDOLPH, Roy, F.; 1; M; White; IN; IL; OH; - ; Nov; Unknown; Hillsboro.

CUMMINGS, Carrie E.; 31; F; White; GA; Scotland; GA; - ; April; Child Birth; Hillsboro.

FANNING, C. B.; 36; M; White; AL; SC; SC; Farmer; July; Consumption; Hillsboro.

GROVES, A.; 1; F; White; FL; NC; GA; - ; Nov; Malarial Fever; Hillsboro.

FRANKLIN, Geo; 63; M; White; FL; GA; - ; Far; Sept; Dropsy; Hillsboro.

McLIN, P. N.; 82; M; White; SC; Ireland; Ireland; Farmer; Feb; Paralysis; Hillsboro.

YATES, JR., James; 1; M; White; FL; GA; FL; - ; Sept; Dysentery; Hillsboro.

WELLS, R. M.; 3; F; White; FL; MS; FL; - ; May; Congestion Brain; Hillsboro.

BURTS, Robt.; 5; M; White; FL; IL; FL; - ; Mar; Congestion; Hillsboro.

PLATT, Peter; 82; M; White; NC; - ; - ; Farmer; July; Old Age; Hillsboro.

WALLS, Margaret; 1; R; White; FL; GA; FL; - ; Sept; Flu; Hillsboro.

SMITH, Zettie N.; 26; F; White; GA; GA; GA; - ; Dec; Flu; Hillsboro.

PLATT, D. P.; 34; F; White; FL; GA; GA; - ; Sept; Congestion Brain; Hillsboro.

McLIN, R. M.; 88; M; White; SC; SC; GA; Farmer; Feb; Paralysis; Hillsboro.

REGISTER, M. J.; 20; F; White; FL; GA; FL; - ; Dec; Dropsy; Hillsboro.

HAWKINS, Leon H.; 5; M; White; FL; FL; FL; - ; Oct; Dysentery; Hillsboro.

HAWKINS, Jno.; 30; M; White; FL; SC; SC; Farmer; Mary; Consumption; Hillsboro.

MARTIN, M. M.; 11; F; White; FL; AL; FL; - ; July; Congestive fever; Hillsboro.

Name; Age; Sex; Race; Born; FABorn; MOBorn;
           Occup; DODeath; Cause Of Death; County

RANSOME, B. B.; 74; M; White; GA; VA; VA; Farmer; Nov;
    Consumption; Hillsboro.
RANSOME, M. B.; 64; M; White; AL; VA; - ; Farmer; April;
    Inflam/bowels; Hillsboro.
PAARTZ, Henry; 14; M; White; Germany; Germany; Germany;
    Farmer; Mar; Accident; Hillsboro.
PAARTZ, Willie; 8; M; White; MO; Germany; Germany; Farmer;
    May; Accident; Hillsboro.
ELLERBEE, J. N.; 5; M; White; AL; GA; FL; - ; June; Unknown;
    Hillsboro.
KNIGHT, E. K.; 18; M; White; NY; NY; CT; - ; Oct; Typhoid
    Fever; Hillsboro.
HANNA, Jane; 61; F; White; TN; NC; NC; - ; Feb; Spinal
    Infection; Hillsboro.
HAZEN, A. E. ; 1; M; White; MO; IA; IL; - ; April; Dropsy;
    Hillsboro.
LENNENT, S. E.; 2; F; White; FL; PA; SC; - ; July; Dysentery;
    Hillsboro.
MURIEL, E. S.; 42; M; White; NY; MA; MA; Machinist; Mar;
    Insanity; Hillsboro.
CRANDON, Cully; 2; M; White; FL; MS; MS; - ; Oct; Malarial
    Fever; Hillsboro.
COLLINS, Julia F.; 39; F; White; GA; GA; GA; - ; Mar; Died
    suddenly; Hillsboro.
DIXON, M. E.; 37; F; White; FL; AL; GA; - ; Feb; Child Birth;
    Hillsboro.
SENSENCY (?), F. J.; 28; M; White; VA; VA; VA; Shoemaker;
    Nov; Consumption; Hillsboro.
MAYO, W. P.; 68; M; White; SC; VA; SC; M. D.; Jan; Typhoid
    Fever; Hillsboro.
PAYNE, E. M.; 43; F; White; MA; ME; ME; - ; April;
    Cancer/stomach; Hillsboro.
WILLIAMS, J. A. J.; 26; M; White; AL; AL; AL; Farmer; Feb;
    Dropsy; Hillsboro.
MOFFETT, E. P. L.; 6; M; White; IN; IN; TN; - ; June;
    Dysentery; Hillsboro.
DeCHENIVA, Amanda; 41; F; White; OH; NY; NY; - ; Nov;
    Rheumatism; Hillsboro.

BURNETTE, Michel; 8; M; White; AL; FL; FL; - ; July; Dropsy; Hillsboro.

HUGGINS, M. C.; 48; F; White; GA; GA; GA; Housewife; July; Inflam/bowels; Holmes

HUGGINS, J. A.; 6; M; White; FL; SC; - ; - ; Sept; Bilious Fever; Holmes

CLEMMONS, J. J.; 37; M; White; GA; GA; GA; Farmer; May; Hemorrhage lungs; Holmes

CURRY, Samuel; 78; M; White; GA; VA; VA; Machinist; Sept; Erysipelas; Holmes

HAMSON, Wm.; 40; M; White; IN; IN; IN; Engineer; Nov; Pneumonia; Holmes

BLACKMON, Ellison; 75; M; White; FL; SC; SC; Farmer; May; Dropsy; Holmes

KITTRAL, Cravin; 34; M; White; FL; GA; AL; Farmer; Mar; Consumption; Holmes

BOWERS, Crocket; 1; M; White; FL; GA; AL; - ; Mar; Burner; Holmes

GLOVER, Margaret C.; 33; F; White; NC; NC; NC; Housewife; Aug; Hemorrhage lungs; Holmes

CANNON, T. W.; 50; M; White; GA; - ; - ; Laborer; May; Murdered; Holmes

WILLIAMS, Joe; 25; M; Black; AL; - ; - ; - ; Dec; Hemorrhage; Holmes

RAMSEY, G. W.; 2; M; White; FL; FL; FL; - ; March; Pneumonia; Holmes

FLOWERS, Georgiana; 12; F; White; AL; AL; GA; - ; July; Dropsy; Holmes

HEWETT, Elizebeth; 58; F; White; AL; NC; NC; Housewife; Aug; Ulcer of throat; Holmes

LEAVINS, Elijah; 70; M; White; GA; NC; NC; Farmer; Jan; Intestines; Holmes

BUSBEY, M. L.; 11; F; White; FL; FL; AL; - ; July; Flux; Holmes

THOMAS, Lem B.; 8; M; White; AL; AL; GA; ; Jan; Congestion; Jackson

ALLEN, E. M.; 26; M; White; FL; SC; GA; Farmer; Nov; Typhoid Fever; Jackson

Name; Age; Sex; Race; Born; FABorn; MOBorn;
              Occup; DODeath; Cause Of Death; County

LAND, Sarah; 84; F; White; GA; NC; NC; - ; Mar; Bronchitis;
    Jackson
SEAY, Wm J.; 1; F; Mu; SC; NC; Ireland; Wheelwright; Dec;
    Pneumonia; Jackson
GRIFFIN, Baby; 1; F; Black; FL; GA; FL; - ; Dec; Fever; Jackson
JONES, Baby; 1; M; Black; FL; FL; FL; - ; Mar; Strangled;
    Jackson
SMITH, Jerry; 42; M; Black; FL; FL; FL; Farmer; July; Dropsy;
    Jackson
PORTER, June; 70; M; Black; VA; VA; VA; Farmer; - ;
    Pneumonia; Jackson
PITMAN, Nathaneal; 4; M; Black; FL; NC; FL; - ; - ; Remittent
    Fever; Jackson
COLLINS, Hulda; 28; F; Black; FL; FL; FL; Laborer; April;
    Dropsy; Jackson
WYNN, Baby; 1; F; Black; FL; FL; FL; - ; April; Fever; Jackson
JORDAN, Robt.; 4; M; Black; FL; FL; FL; - ; Sept; Remittent
    Fever; Jackson
WEBB, Walter; 22; M; Black; FL; NC; FL; Timberhand; Jan;
    Dropsy; Jackson
RUSS, Peggy; 81; F; Black; NC; NC; SC; - ; April; Old Age;
    Jackson
GARRELL (?), H. M.; 23; F; White; FL; NC; AL; Housewife;
    April; Unknown; Jackson
McNEALY, E. L.; 20; M; White; FL; FL; GA; Farmer; April;
    Blood Poisoning; Jackson
SIMS, Adeline; 26; F; White; FL; SC; Fla; Housewife; May;
    Unknown; Jackson
WILSON (?), Jesse; 67; M; White; TN; - ; - ; Farmer; Oct;
    Congestion bowels; Jackson
DOOLEY (?), Sarah; 22; F; Black; FL; FL; FL; Housewife; May;
    Unknown; Jackson
PELT, Martin; 2; M; Black; FL; FL; FL; - ; April; Dropsy;
    Jackson
SIMS, Jacob; 56; M; Black; NC; - ; NC; Farmer; Dec; Bilious
    Fever; Jackson
STEWART, Clarence; 1; M; White; FL; FL; FL; - ; Feb;
    Unknown; Jackson

FOLSOM, Chestley; 83; M; White; NC; NC; - ; Farmer; July;
Intermittent Fever; Jackson

BULLOCK, Sandy; 2; M; Black; FL; FL; FL; - ; Feb; Burned;
Jackson

POTTER, James; 1; M; Mu; FL; FL; FL; - ; Feb; Bled to death;
Jackson

WHITE, Susan; 20; F; White; FL; FL; FL; Housewife; April;
Child Bed; Jackson

BAKER, Harriet; 60; F; Black; TN; - ; - ; Housewife; June;
Bilious Fever; Jackson

SIMS, Addie; 26; F; White; FL; SC; AL; Housewife; Aug; Child
Bed; Jackson

SIMSON, Peggie; 26; F; Black; FL; FL; FL; Farmer; May;
Dropsy; Jackson

DENINS, Infant; 1; F; Black; FL; GA; FL; - ; June; Unknown;
Jackson

PICKRED, Infant; 1; F; White; FL; LA; MS; - ; Jan; Unknown;
Jackson

PICKRED, Ja. R.; 2; M; White; LA; LA; MS; - ; Aug; Congestion
Brain; Jackson

DAWSON, Viola; 2; F; Black; FL; FL; FL; - ; June; Continued
Fever; Jackson

KING, Littleton; 78; M; White; SC; SC; SC; Farmer; Dec;
Apoplexy; Jackson

BEE, Delia; 18; F; Black; FL; FL; GA; - ; May; Dropsy; Jackson

JOHNSON, Rebecca; 34; F; White; FL; FL; FL; Farmer; Jan;
Pneumonia; Jackson

JOHNSON, D.; 18; M; White; FL; FL; FL; - ; Feb; Pneumonia;
Jackson

JOHNSON, John; 32; M; White; FL; FL; FL; - ; Feb; Pneumonia;
Jackson

WHIDDON, Johnnie; 1; F; White; FL; GA; FL; - ; Sept;
Congestion; Jackson

MIKLES, Henry; 46; M; Black; GA; NC; NC; Laborer; Feb;
Dropsy; Jackson

SLOAN, Tilda; 2; F; White; FL; GA; FL; - ; May; Congestion;
Jackson

Name; Age; Sex; Race; Born; FABorn; MOBorn;
          Occup; DODeath; Cause Of Death; County

EDWARDS, Patty J.; 1; F; White; FL; GA; GA; - ; June;
    Convulsions; Jackson
SLOAN, Sallie; 55; F; White; GA; GA; GA; - ; Sept; Congestive
    chill; Jackson
BROGDEN, Ada; 17; F; White; FL; FL; FL; - ; Aug; Child Birth;
    Jackson
THOMAS, Pick; 7; M; Black; FL; GA; GA; - ; April; Pneumonia;
    Jackson
ROBENSON, Julia P.; 24; F; Mu; FL; GA; GA; Laborer; March;
    Pneumonia; Jackson
WILSON, Mary; 2; F; Black; GA; FL; GA; - ; Aug; Fever;
    Jackson
ROBENSON, Laura; 1; M; Mu; FL; FL; FL; - ; April;
    Convulsions; Jackson
SHERMAN, Manual; 45; M; Black; GA; GA; GA; Laborer; Mar;
    Pneumonia; Jackson
HEWITT, Nelson; 13; M; White; FL; NC; SC; Laborer; April;
    Diarrhea; Jackson
McDANIEL, Frank ; 30; M; White; FL; GA; GA; - ; July; Shot to
    death; Jackson
McDANIEL, Council; 20; M; White; FL; GA; GA; - ; July;
    Unknown; Jackson
MITCHEL, J. W.; - ; M; White; SC; SC; - ; - ; Oct; Dropsy;
    Jackson
NICHOLS, C. M.; 16; M; White; FL; GA; FL; - ; April; Dropsy;
    Jackson
CONNELLY, Henry H.; 14; M; White; FL; GA; GA; - ; Sept;
    Congestion bowels; Jackson
SEXTON, Edward; 5; M; White; FL; GA; AL; - ; July;
    Congestion bowels; Jackson
WHITE, Laurence; 1; M; White; FL; FL; FL; - ; Feb; Cramp
    Colic; Jackson
HODGES, B.; 4; F; White; AL; GA; FL; - ; Sept; Diptheria;
    Jackson
BOONE, A. I. V.; 2; F; White; FL; FL; FL; - ; Oct; Typhoid
    Fever; Jackson
PYKE, Julia; 59; F; White; SC; SC; SC; Housewife; April;
    Cancer/stomach; Jackson

WILLIAMS, Julia W.; 40; F; White; NC; NC; NC; - ; Mar;
Pneumonia; Jackson

HUNTER, M.; 40; F; Black; SC; GA; GA; - ; Jan; [?]bowels;
Jackson

HARRISON,[unattainable]; 85; F; Black; FL; - ; - ; Laborer; Sept;
Heart Disease; Jefferson

FORD, [unattainable]; 1; F; Black; FL; FL; FL; - ; June; Diarrhea;
Jefferson

BLACK [-----], [unattainable]; 1; M; Black; FL; FL; FL; - ; Sept;
Unknown; Jefferson

BLUNT, [unattainable]; 51; F; White; GA; GA; GA; - ; Jan;
Cholic; Jefferson

STROMMAN, [unattainable]; 60; M; Black; FL; FL; FL; - ; June;
Dropsy; Jefferson

RHODE, [unattainable]; 1; F; White; FL; FL; FL; - ; April;
Congestion Brain; Jefferson

GREEN, L; 35; F; White; FL; FL; FL; - ; June; Consumption;
Jefferson

SHERMAN, R.; 60; M; White; GA; GA; GA; Farmer; May;
Consumption; Jefferson

GREEN, Ann; 70; F; White; SC; SC; SC; Farmer; Nov;
Congestion; Jefferson

SHERMAN, Ellis; 35; M; Black; GA; GA; GA; Farmer; July;
Consumption; Jefferson

ADKINSON, Robert; 4; M; White; FL; GA; FL; Farmer; July;
Bilious Fever; Jefferson

GRAHAM, Peggie; 35; F; White; GA; GA; GA; Farmer; July;
Bilious Fever; Jefferson

C [unknown], Rachel; 50; F; White; FL; GA; GA; - ; Jan; Heart
Disease; Jefferson

JOHNSON, H. Julia; 43; F; White; FL; GA; GA; - ; Sept;
Unknown; Jefferson

GRAHAM, Arthur; 56; M; Black; FL; FL; FL; Laborer; May;
Dysentery; Jefferson

TAYLOR, M. B.; 48; F; White; FL; FL; FL; - ; May; Congestion;
Jefferson

ALLEN, Lewis; 42; M; White; GA; GA; GA; Laborer; May;
Dysentery; Jefferson

Name; Age; Sex; Race; Born; FABorn; MOBorn;
        Occup; DODeath; Cause Of Death; County

LIGHTSEY, D. E.; 20; M; White; FL; SC; FL ; Sectioin [?]; Jan;
    Typhoid Fever; Jefferson
WALKER, Amanda; 34; F; White; FL; GA; GA; Housewife;
    April; Typhoid Fever; Jefferson
LEWIS, Julia; 1; F; Black; FL; FL; FL; - ; July; Dysentery;
    Jefferson
NAME MISSING; 95; F; Black; SC; SC; NY; Midwife; July;
    Dropsy; Jefferson
TARRELL; 60; M; Black; GA; GA; GA; - ; April; Dropsy;
    Jefferson
RODGERS; 5; M; White; FL; FL; FL; - ; Nov; Congestion;
    Jefferson
RODGERS; 1; M; White; FL; FL; FL; - ; Nov; Cholera Infection;
    Jefferson
RODGERS, F. J.; 3; F; White; FL; GA; FA; - ; June; Pneumonia;
    Jefferson
ADAM,; 6; F; White; FL; GA; GA; - ; May; Gen. Congestion ;
    Jefferson
HAMRICK, W. A. ; 1; M; White; FL; SC; GA; - ; July;
    Congestion Brain; Jefferson
FRANKLING, John; 3; M; Black; FL; FL; FL; - ; Aug;
    Congestion; Jefferson
GRUMBALDT,; 18; M; Black; GA; GA; SC; W. D.; Feb; Kidney
    Disease; Jefferson
MOSELY, Caroline; - ; F; Mu; AL; AL; AL; ; Oct; Dropsy;
    Jefferson
GELDER, John; 2; M; White; FL; FL; FL; - ; Oct; Pneumonia;
    Jefferson
INFANT; - ; M; Black; FL; FL; FL; - ; Jan; Stillborn; Jefferson
WILLIS, Laura; 38; F; White; FL; Fl; GA; - ; Feb; Pneumonia;
    Jefferson
BELLAMY, Aliza; 37; F; Black; GA; GA; GA; - ; Nov;
    Unknown; Jefferson
GELIA, Martin; 84; M; Black; SC; SC; SC; Laborer; Jan; Heart
    Disease; Jefferson
G [----], Archer; 2; M; Mu; FL; FL; FL; - ; Sept; Fever; Jefferson
WASHINGTON, Jack; 65; M; Black; NC; NC; NC; Laborer; Oct;
    White Swelling; Jefferson

HIGHTOWER, Jesse; 73; M; White; SC; SC; SC; Farmer; Aug;
Bladder Disease; Jefferson

AMOS, Minnie; 1; F; Black; FL; FL; FL; - ; March; Unknown;
Jefferson

RUSS, GeorgeAnn; 11; F; Black; FL; FL; FL; - ; June; Unknown;
Jefferson

HIGGINS, Louisa; 1; F; Black; FL; FL; FL; - ; April; Unknown;
Jefferson

KIRBY, Sallie; 1; F; Black; FL; FL; FL; - ; June; Unknown;
Jefferson

CHRISTOPHER, Ann; 84; F; White; FL; GA; GA; Farmer;
March; Old Age; Jefferson

COBB, Milton; 4; M; Black; FL; SC; SC; - ; March; Pneumonia;
Jefferson

ANDERSON, John; 1; M; Black; FL; FL; FL; - ; July; Thrush;
Jefferson

HARRIS, Hanson; 5; M; Mu; FL; FL; FL; - ; Sept; Worms;
Jefferson

LINTON, M. A.; 39; F; White; FL; SC; SC; - ; March; Fever;
Jefferson

BROOKINS, Ben; 30; F; Black; SC; SC; SC; - ; April; Dysentery;
Jefferson

PARRISH, Sam; 70; M; Black; SC; SC; SC; Farmer; April;
Pneumonia; Jefferson

BROOKS, Lot; 26; M; Black; FL; SC; FL; Teacher; Aug; Brain
Fever; Jefferson

SHAW, George; 38; M; Black; LA; LA; LA; Farmer; May;
Typhoid Fever; Jefferson

COY, E. A.; 58; M; White; NC; NC; NC; Farmer; Feb;
Consumption; Jefferson

HARRIS, Nancy; 90; F; Black; VA; VA; VA; - ; May;
Pneumonia; Jefferson

McGUIRE, G. H.; 13; F; Black; FL; VA; VA; - ; Aug;
[unreadable]; Jefferson

BUTLER, Viny; 72; F; Black; SC; SC; SC; - ; Nov; Consumption;
Jefferson

BUTLER, Chambers; 23; M; Black; FL; SC; SC; Farmer; April;
Consumption; Jefferson

Name; Age; Sex; Race; Born; FABorn; MOBorn;
Occup; DODeath; Cause Of Death; County

BROOKS, Rachel; 69; F; Black; SC; SC; SC; Farmer; May;
Dropsy; Jefferson
COLSON, J. A.; 21; M; White; FL; GA; GA; Farmer; April;
Perocardilie; Jefferson
WILLIAMS, Lizzie; 86; F; Black; FL; GA; GA; - ; Nov; Dropsy;
Jefferson
McKINNY, Sam; 30; M; Black; GA; GA; GA; Farmer; July;
Dysentery; Jefferson
GRAHAM, Noah; 72; M; Black; VA; VA; VA; Farmer; May;
Dropsy; Jefferson
GATHER, Archer; 2; M; Mu; FL; FL; FL; - ; Sept; Fever;
Jefferson
GOODWIN, Temple; 19; F; Black; GA; GA; GA; Laborer; Dec;
Asthma; Jefferson
STRAUS, Eddie; 50; M; Black; FL; GA; FL; - ; May; Dropsy;
Jefferson
WRIGHT, A.; 5; M; Black; FL; FL; FL; - ; Oct; Dropsy; Jefferson
HENRY, Wm. ; 23; M; Black; SC; SC; SC; Farmer; - ;
Pneumonia; Jefferson
CARLISLE, W. W. (infant of); 1; - ; - ; - ; - ; - ; - ; - ; - ; - ; '
CONNELL, Lula V.; 2; F; White; FL; FL; FL; - ; Sept; Brain
Fever; Jefferson
CONNELL, M. B.; 1; F; White; FL; FL; FL; - ; March;
Pneumonia; Jefferson
HAYNES, C. T.; 27; F; White; FL; FL; FL; Mother; Feb; Dropsy;
Jefferson
BRAMLET, Thos.; 1; M; White; FL; SC; FL; ; June; General
Fever; Jefferson
SAMUEL, Mariah; 12; F; Black; GA; GA; GA; Laborer; May;
Congestion; Jefferson
CASADY, J. W. ; 62; M; White; FL; Ireland; GA; Farmer; May;
Dropsy; Jefferson
KILPATRICK, Mathew; 1; M; Mu; FL; FL; NC; - ; Sept; Thrash;
Jefferson
TAYLOR, Doctor; 8; M; Black; FL; FL; FL; - ; July; Dropsy;
Jefferson
TAYLOR, G. W.; 6; M; Black; FL; FL; FL; - ; Jan; Congestion
Brain; Jefferson

TAYLOR, Dora; 17; F; Black; FL; FL; FL; Laborer; Jan; Milk
Leg; Jefferson

HAWKINS, Millie; 18; F; Black; FL; FL; FL; Laborer; Feb;
Dropsy; Jefferson

HAWKINS, Scilla; 20; F; Mu; FL; VA; VA; Laborer; Feb;
Congestion; Jefferson

BUCK, Thor[n]ton; 76; M; Mu; VA; FL; VA; Mechanic; Oct;
Congestion; Jefferson

JOICE, Abram; 65; M; Black; FL; VA; VA; Farmer; Oct;
Pneumonia; Jefferson

WIGGINS, Manuel; 6; M; Black; FL; VA; FL; - ; Jan;
Congestion; Jefferson

REED, Andy; 85; M; Black; SC; FL; SC; - ; Sept; Old Age;
Jefferson

BOYD, Clara; 1; F; Black; FL; SC; SC; - ; Aug; Worms; Jefferson

JERKINS, Sophy; 80; F; Black; SC; GA; SC; - ; Dec; Epilepsy;
Jefferson

DONALDSON, Emma; 20; F; Black; FL; SC; FL; Laborer; Jan;
Child Bed; Jefferson

HILL, Scinda; 36; F; Black; GA; GA; GA; Laborer; Sept; Cancer;
Jefferson

GRANTHAM, Pink; 5; M; White; FL; FL; FL; - ; Oct; Liver
Complaint; Jefferson

GIVENS, Infant P.; 1; M; Black; FL; SC; FL; - ; March; Mother's
health; Jefferson

SAUNDERS, W J. (Infant); 1; M; Black; FL; FL; FL; - ; March;
Pneumonia; Jefferson

JORDAN, Infant C.; 1; M; Black; FL; GA; FL; - ; April; Mother's
health; Jefferson

BRYANT, Wm.; 1; M; Black; FL; FL; FL; - ; June; Diarrhea;
Jefferson

SCRUGS, Sam; 65; M; Black; NC; NC; NC; Laborer; Jan;
Dropsy; Jefferson

PERKINS, Simon; 60; M; Mu; NC; NC; NC; Farmer; July;
Typhoid Fever; Jefferson

BUTLER, Clem; 65; M; Black; FL; GA; GA; Laborer; July;
Typhoid Fever; Jefferson

NEIL, John; 110; M; Black; SC; SC; SC; Laborer; July; Old Age;
Jefferson

MILLER, Lizzetta; 85; F; Mu; SC; SC; SC; Servant; Oct;
Congestion lungs; Jefferson

C(unreadable), Emma; 28; F; Black; FL; AL; AL; Laborer; July;
unknown; Jefferson

BAKER, Mary; 65; F; Black; VA; VA; VA; Cook; Dec; Pleurisy;
Jefferson

WHEELER, Ada; 18; F; White; FL; FL; FL; - ; Sept; Child bed
fever; Jefferson

H (unreadable), Gail; 19; M; Black; FL; FL; FL; - ; June; Burn
infection; Jefferson

DAVIS, Pat; 18; M; Mu; FL; VA; VA; Laborer; May; Typhoid
Fever; Jefferson

ARMSTRONG, Rosa; 14; F; Black; FL; FL; FL; - ; Feb; Typhoid
Fever; Jefferson

VICUS, Bessa; 39; F; Black; GA; GA; GA; - ; July; Congestion;
Jefferson

HENRY, Davy; 57; M; Black; NC; GA; GA; Farmer; July;
Unknown; Jefferson

HUTSON, Juley; 12; F; Black; FL; FL; FL; - ; - ; Unknown;
Jefferson

JOHNSON, Melissa; 1; F; Black; FL; FL; FL; - ; April;
Pneumonia; Jefferson

BALDY, Wm. C.; 58; M; White; GA; GA; GA; Farmer; April;
Pneumonia; Jefferson

BARROW, Viney; 60; F; Black; SC; SC; SC; Laborer; Dec;
Burnt; Jefferson

PUSHA, Samuel; 35; M; Black; FL; SC; SC; Laborer; April;
Dropped Dead; Jefferson

McDAVID, [unreadable]; 3; M; Black; FL; FL; FL; - ; Sept;
Typhoid Fever; Jefferson

ALLEN, Benj.; 11; M; Black; FL; FL; SC; Laborer; Oct; Heart
Disease; Jefferson

CLEAR, Sally; 3; F; Mu; FL; FL; FL; - ; Dec; Typhoid Fever;
Jefferson

SMITH, Mary F.; 10; F; White; GA; AL; GA; Scholar; July;
Congestion; Jefferson

JOHNSON, Racheal; 20; F; Black; SC; SC; SC; Domestic; June; Continuous fever; Jefferson

HAWKINS, Nancy; 74; F; Black; FL; SC; SC; Field Hand; Feb; Dropsy; Jefferson

LOVETT, Andrew; 65; M; Black; SC; SC; SC; Baskets; Nov; Ulcer of leg; Jefferson

GREEN, Wm.; 110; M; Black; NC; NC; NC; Farmer; May; Old Age; Jefferson

McCURDY, Phillip; 17; M; Black; FL; FL; FL; Domestic; Feb; Dropsy; Jefferson

FINLEY, Lizzie; 25; F; White; FL; FL; AL; Domestic; May; Liver Complaint; Jefferson

ANDREWS, Sarah; 24; F; Black; FL; FL; FL; Field Hand; July; Dropsy; Jefferson

HOWARD, Henry; 5; M; Black; FL; FL; SC; - ; Feb; Typhoid Fever; Jefferson

HOWARD, Henderson; 4; M; Black; FL; FL; FL; - ; Feb; Congestion; Jefferson

STEWART, Fanny; 24; F; Black; FL; FL; FL; Laundress; Mar; Pneumonia; Leon

DORSEY, John Wesley; 1; M; Black; FL; FL; Fl; - ; Jan; Brain Disease; Leon

DORSEY, Starling; 2; M; Black; FL; FL; FL; - ; Oct; Brain Disease; Leon

HERNDON, Baby; 2; M; Black; FL; FL; FL; - ; June; Brain Disease; Leon

EVANS, Robert; 37; M; Mu; FL; GA; GA; Painter; Sept; Typhoid Fever; Leon

COOPER, Ephraim; 47; M; Black; FL; NC; SC; Carpenter; Mar; Pneumonia; Leon

TURNER, George; 3; M; Black; FL; FL; FL; - ; Aug; Spasms; Leon

ROBERTSON, Edmund; 44; M; Black; FL; VA; VA; Teamster; May; Lung Disease; Leon

[Child]; 1; M; Black; FL; FL; FL; - ; Mar; Debility; Leon

PEPPER, James; 37; M; Black; GA; GA; GA; Butcher; May; Pneumonia; Leon

SMITH, Lydia G.; 63; F; Mu; FL; - ; SC; Teacher; Aug; Abs of
    stomach; Leon
SMITH, Noah H.; 41; M; Black; FL; MD; VA; Farmer; April;
    Pneumonia; Leon
JONES, Geo. H.; 24; M; Black; FL; NC; NC; Porter; May;
    Crushed to death; Leon
JACKSON, Brian; 1; M; Black; FL; FL; GA; - ; June; Brain
    Fever; Leon
SMITH, A. P.; 53; M; Black; NY; NY; NY; Com. Trade; Sept;
    Bowel Disease; Leon
BULL, Dalceida; 83; F; White; France; France; France; - ; Nov;
    Decay; Leon
CAMPBELL, Hannah; 70; F; Black; GA; GA; GA; Cook; May;
    Stroke; Leon
WHITFIELD, JR., R. A.; 23; M; Black; NC; NC; AL; Farmer;
    Mar; Pneumonia; Leon
CHRISTMAS, Alice; 17; F; Mu; NC; NC; NC; Seamstress; Feb;
    Hemorrhage; Leon
SHINE, John A.; 27; M; Black; FL; FL; FL; Lawyer; May;
    Dysentery; Leon
WILLIAMS, Rachel; 24; F; Black; FL; NC; NC; Cook; Jan; Child
    Birth; Leon
PRATORIUS, J.; 69; M; White; - ; Germany; Germany; Tailor;
    Aug; Hernia; Leon
WILLIAMS, Laura; 24; F; White; GA; GA; GA; Seamstress; Feb;
    Typhoid Fever; Leon
NIX, Delphi; 2; F; Black; FL; FL; FL; - ; July; Poisoned; Leon
Nix, Barney; 1; M; Black; FL; FL; LF; - ; July; Poisoned; Leon
BARRS, L. E.; 26; F; White; FL; NY; FL; Housekeep; Feb;
    Pneumonia; Leon
BARRS, John A.; 15; M; White; FL; GA; FL; Laborer; Feb;
    Complications; Leon
BARRS, Arthur; 1; M; White; FL; GA; FL; - ; Sept;
    Complications; Leon
CRICHLOW, Amanda; 47; F; White; FL; TN; SC; Housekeep;
    May; Consumption; Leon
JONES, Mary; 70; F; Black; GA; GA; GA; Laborer; Jan; Decay;
    Leon

HAWKINS, Wm. Henry; 29; M; Black; FL; NC; KY; Cook; Aug;
Drowned; Leon
STAFFOLD, Isaac; 35; M; Black; AL; AL; AL; Farmer; Aug;
Dropsy; Leon
HILL, Richard; 35; M; Black; FL; VA; VA; Laborer; Sept;
Pneumonia; Leon
RANDOLPH, A. L.; 36; M; White; FL; VA; NC; Physician; July;
Consumption; Leon
KWILECKI, M.; 32; M; White; Germany; Germany; Germany;
Merchant; Nov; Brain Fever; Leon
FAIRBANKS, Andrew; 35; M; White; FL; ME; FL; Conductor;
Dec; Menningitis; Leon
BYRD, W. P.; 26; M; White; Fl; FL; NC; Lawyer; Aug; Malarial
Fever; Leon
Baby; 1; M; White; FL; FL; FL; - ; Sept; - ; Leon
G [unreadable], Alex; - ; M; White; GA; TN; FL; - ; April; Croup;
Leon
MOON, Alex; 33; M; Black; FL; VA; VA; Barber; Feb; - ; Leon
BRYANT, Gomer; 70; M; Black; NC; NC; NC; Minister; Dec;
Pneumonia; Leon
COOK, Henry; 1; M; White; FL; FL; FL; - ; Sept; Bowel Disease;
Leon
WILSON, Clifford; 1; M; White; FL; FL; FL; - ; Aug; - ; Leon
[unreadable], Hattie; 42; F; Black; FL; NC; NC; Cook; Sept; Ulcer
of Stomach; Leon
GILES, Josephine; 1; F; Black; FL; FL; FL; - ; Aug; Diarrhea;
Leon
WELLES, Belle; 25; F; Mu; FL; FL; FL; Seamstress; Aug; - ;
Leon
WILLIAMS, Priscilla; 73; F; Black; GA; GA; GA; Cook; Mar;
Decay; Leon
JACKSON, Henry; 23; M; Black; AL; NC; NC; Farm hand; July;
Crushed to death; Leon
RANDALL, Abbie; 68; F; Black; NC; NC; NC; Cook; Mar;
Decay; Leon
DENT, Julia; 25; F; Mu; FL; SC; FL; - ; Dec; Typhoid Fever;
Leon

KNIGHT, Adeline; 50; F; Black; FL; SL; NC; Housewife; Sept;
    Dropsy; Leon
HANSON, Clarissa; 3; F; Black; FL; FL; FL; - ; Oct; Kidney
    Disease; Leon
WOODWARD, Mach; 2; M; Black; FL; FL; FL; - ; Aug;
    Congestion; Leon
WOODWARD, Baby; 1; F; Black; FL; FL; FL; - ; Feb; Stillborn;
    Leon
BRYANT, Elizabeth; 1; F; Black; FL; NC; FL; - ; June; Teething;
    Leon
HAWKINS, Jesse; 1; M; Black; FL; FL; FL; - ; May; Pneumonia;
    Leon
WILLIAMS, Robert; 1; M; Mu; FL; Fl; FL; - ; July; - ; Leon
ADAMS, Mathew; 14; M; Black; FL; FL; FL; Laborer; Jan; - ;
    Leon
STUBBS, Elizabeth; 49; F; Black; FL; Fl; Fl; Laborer; Dec; - ;
    Leon
STEFFER (?), Elizabeth; 63; F; Mu; FL; - ; - ; Laborer; Jan;
    Pneumonia; Leon
BOATWRIGHT, J. L.; 50; M; White; FL; FL; FL; Butcher; July;
    Pneumonia; Leon
BOATWRIGHT, Mary; 45; F; White; FL; FL; FL; - ; Mar;
    Pneumonia; Leon
WILSON, Charity; 2; F; Black; FL; FL; FL; - ; Aug; Worms;
    Leon
ADAMS, Martha; 19; F; White; FL; GA; GA; - ; Jan; Child Birth;
    Leon
GIBBONS, Nancy C.; 5; F; White; FL; GA; FL; - ; Aug; Brain
    Fever; Leon
CHANDLER, John; 1; M; Black; FL; GA; FL; - ; Jan; Diptheria;
    Leon
KELLY, Lillian; 1; F; White; FL; FL; FL; - ; April; Cholera
    Infection; Leon
KELLY, Angus H.; 3; M; White; FL; FL; FL; - ; July; Bilious
    Fever; Leon
BRAMLETT, Misouri; 17; F; White; AL; AL; AL; - ; May;
    Dropsy; Leon

CHAIRS, Douglas; 2; M; White; FL; FL; - ; - ; Nov; Congestion;
Leon
LINDSEY, Mariah; 35; F; N; FL; - ; FL; - ; Laborer; Dropsy;
Leon
WILLIAMS, David; 7; M; Black; FL; FL; FL; - ; Jan; Pneumonia;
Leon
JOHNSON, Louisa; 1; F; Black; FL; FL; FL; - ; Aug; Congestion;
Leon
DECORCIS, Mimi; 58; F; White; France; France; France; Farmer;
April; Pneumonia; Leon
LEVY, H. C.; 44; M; White; FL; NC; FL; Farmer; Mar;
Pneumonia; Leon
CHAIRS, Green; 69; M; White; GA; GA; GA; Farmer; Feb;
Urinary Infect; Leon
MITCHELL Goodie E,; 21; F; White; GA; FL; GA; - ; July;
Malaria; Leon
HALE, N. L.; 48; M; White; FL; NC; NC; Farmer; Jan; Dropsy;
Leon
FLEMING, C[unreadable]; 23; F; White; Fl; SC; SC; - ; Dec;
Pneumonia; Leon
HOPKINS, Green B.; 50; M; White; FL; GA; GA; Farmer; Jan;
Pneumonia; Leon
ROBERTSON, W. F.; 72; M; White; VA; VA; VA; Physician;
Jan; Pneumonia; Leon
CRAIG, John A.; 48; M; White; MD; MD; MD; Farmer; July;
Pneumonia; Leon
HOLLOWAY, Abram; 55; M; Black; NC; NC; NC; Laborer; Jan;
Gen. Debility; Leon
HOLLOWAY, Allice; 19; F; Black; FL; NC; FL; Laborer; Feb;
Pneumonia; Leon
LEON, Robert; 45; M; Black; NC; NC; NC; Laborer; May;
Pneumonia; Leon
CRAWLEY, Rebecca; 11; F; Black; FL; FL; FL; - ; May;
Convulsions; Leon
THOMPSON, Daniel; 1; M; Black; FL; FL; FL; - ; July;
Convulsions; Leon
BURGESS, Nazareth; 1; M; Black; FL; FL; FL; - ; June;
Convulsions; Leon

WILLIAMS, Frank; 60; M; Black; FL; SC; SC; Laborer; May;
    Dropsy; Leon
HAMMOND, Ann; 1; F; Black; FL; FL; FL; - ; April; Whooping
    cough; Leon
STEWART, Malinda; 1; F; Black; FL; FL; FL; - ; Mar; - ; Leon
JACKSON, Hessie; 20; F; Black; FL; FL; FL; Laborer; Mar;
    Child Birth; Leon
BURNY, Infant; 1; F; Black; FL; FL; FL; - ; Feb; Whooping
    cough; Leon
HUMPHRIES, Daniel; 2; M; Black; FL; FL; FL; - ; April;
    Pneumonia; Leon
COFIELD, Victoria; 3; F; Black; FL; FL; FL; - ; June; Drowned;
    Leon
DANTZLER, James; 1; M; Black; FL; FL; FL; - ; July; Whooping
    cough; Leon
STRINGER, W. T.; 45; M; White; GA; GA; GA; Farmer; July;
    Pneumonia; Leon
YEOMANS, Susanna; 50; F; Black; FL; FL; FL; Laborer; July;
    Asthma; Leon
HARGER, W. T.; 40; M; White; FL; FL; FL; Farmer; July;
    Congestion Brain; Leon
SMITH, Patrick; 82; M; White; GA; GA; GA; Farmer; Aug; Fell;
    Leon
JACKSON, Lewis; 18; M; Black; FL; FL; FL; Laborer; May;
    Congestion; Leon
THOMPSON, Austin; 52; M; Black; AL; AL; AL; Laborer; Dec;
    Congestion Brain; Leon
THOMPSON, Irene; 50; F; Black; AL; AL; AL; Laborer; Mar;
    Heart Disease; Leon
RUFFIN, John; 50; M; Black; NC; NC; NC; Laborer; Feb;
    Syphylus; Leon
RHODES, Amy; 35; F; Black; SC; SC; SC; Laborer; Jan;
    Syphilitis fever; Leon
FRIERSON, Wilson; 44; M; Black; AL; AL; AL; Laborer; - ;
    Broken Leg; Leon
BEATIE, Allice; 25; F; Black; FL; FL; FL; Laborer; Mar;
    Hemorrhage; Leon

HUTTO, Ola Bell; 4; F; White; FL; FL; FL; - ; June; Congestion
Brain; Leon

ONEAL, John; 1; M; Black; FL; FL; FL; - ; July; Congestion;
Leon

(unknown), Christine; 1; F; White; NC; NC; NC; - ; July; Cholera
Infection; Leon

JONES, Eve; 105; F; Black; NC; NC; NC; Laborer; April; Heart
Disease; Leon

NORMAN, Amanda; 24; F; Black; FL; FL; FL; Laborer; April;
Child Birth; Leon

SWITZER, Charity; 65; F; Black; NC; NC; NC; Laborer; Sept;
Throat Disease; Leon

G[unreadable], James; 27; M; Black; FL; FL; FL; Laborer; Mar;
Pneumonia; Leon

ALDRICH, Mary; 17; F; Black; FL; FL; FL; Laborer; Nov;
Hemorrhage; Leon

BANKS, Margaret; 4; F; Black; FL; FL; FL; - ; Mar; Dropsy;
Leon

BARNY, Clara; 43; F; Black; FL; FL; FL; Laborer; May;
Pneumonia; Leon

[unreadable], Lucien; 1; M; Black; FL; FL; FL; - ; May;
Pneumonia; Leon

SPENCER, Edward; 4; M; Black; FL; FL; FL; - ; Mar;
Pneumonia; Leon

WILLIAMS, Eliza; 62; F; Black; VA; VA; VA; Laborer; Mar;
Congestion Brain; Leon

HURST, Martha; 15; F; Black; FL; FL; FL; Laborer; Jan;
Pneumonia; Leon

HOGAN, Pearl; 1; F; Black; FL; FL; FL; - ; Aug; Dropsy; Leon

DUBART, James; 87; M; Black; VA; VA; VA; Laborer; May;
Dysentery; Leon

HOLMS, Celia; 39; F; Black; FL; FL; FL; Laborer; Jan; Dropped
dead; Leon

FOOTMAN, Julia A.; 25; F; White; SC; SC; SC; - ; Sept; Malarial
Fever; Leon

FOOTMAN, Nettie W.; 1; F; White; FL; FL; LF; - ; Aug; Cholera
Infection; Leon

MITCHELL, Richard A.; 2; M; White; FL; FL; FL; - ; Aug;
    Congestion; Leon
HUNTER, Ann; 43; F; Black; FL; FL; FL; Laborer; Sept;
    Congestive ; Leon
HADSOCK, Veannie; 38; F; White; FL; GA; GA; - ; Feb; - ; Levy
CALHOUN, Thom; 44; M; White; GA; GA; GA; Cooper; June;
    Dropsy; Levy
TERREL, L. Z.; 49; M; White; Ohio; MA; MA; Engineer; Feb;
    Dropsy; Levy
STROBLE, Dan.l; 46; M; White; SC; SC; SC; Blacksmith; Jan;
    Abscess; Levy
WILKERSON, Til (?); 24; M; Black; FL; SC; SC; Teacher; Nov;
    Malarial Fever; Levy
B[unreadable], Mildred; 3; F; White; CT; England; MA; - ; Aug;
    Scarlet Fever; Levy
POPE, M. C.; 34; F; White; TN; NC; NC; - ; June; Malarial Fever;
    Levy
B[unreadable], S. E.; 30; F; White; NH; NH; NH; - ; June; Brain;
    Levy
Infant; - ; M; White; FL; Sweden; Sweden; - ; May; Stillborn;
    Levy
Infant; - ; M; White; FL; FL; FL; - ; Dec; Stillborn; Levy
Infant; - ; F; White; FL; FL; FL; - ; - ; Stillborn; Levy
ALSTON, Sophy; 38; F; Black; FL; NC; NC; ; May; Dropsy;
    Levy
LEE, Infant; 1; F; Black; FL; VA; FL; - ; Dec; Cold; Levy
HODGES, Bertha; 1; F; White; FL; FL; FL; - ; Dec; Teething;
    Levy
HAWKINS, Infant; 1; M; Black; FL; FL; FL; - ; June; Mother laid
    on it; Levy
DANIELS, Jn.; 60; F; Black; VA; VA; VA; - ; Dec; Paralysis;
    Levy
STEVENS, M.; 1; F; Mu; FL; FL; FL; - ; Feb; Fever; Levy
CALE, Infant; 1; M; White; FL; SC; SC; - ; Nov; Spasms; Levy
ORR, Infant; 1; M; White; MS; AL; MS; - ; Dec; - ; Levy
ORR, Infant; 1; M; White; MS; AL; MS; - ; Dec; - ; Levy
ORR, G; 2; M; White; FL; VA; GA; - ; Jan; Inflam/bowels; Levy

DEMARE, Infant; 1; M; White; FL; FL; FL; - ; Aug; Stillborn;
Levy

MARTIN, Patrick; 19; M; Black; FL; FL; FL; - ; Dec; Dysentery;
Levy

STEVENS, Geo.; 1; M; White; FL; GA; FL; - ; June; Dysentery;
Levy

WILLIAMS, R.; 1; M; Black; FL; FL; GA; - ; May; Spasms; Levy

WILLIAMS, Infant; 1; F; Black; FL; FL; GA; - ; Mar; Spasms;
Levy

BARROW, J; 10; F; Black; FL; FL; FL; - ; May; Congestion;
Levy

WINANS, Jns.; 72; M; White; NY; NY; NY; Farmer; Dec; Heat;
Levy

MOORE, H.; 38; F; Black; GA; GA; GA; - ; July; Tumor/Breast;
Levy

WADE, Jn.; 21; F; White; GA; GA; GA; ; Dec; Inflam/bowels;
Levy

BENNETT, Wm.; 67; M; White; SC; SC; SC; Farmer; May;
Dropsy; Levy

FIELDS, Wm.; 68; M; White; AL; AL; AL; - ; Aug; Liver
Complaint; Levy

CAMPBELL, Infant; 1; F; Black; FL; FL; FL; .- ; Aug; Cold; Levy

POPE, Laura; 6; F; Black; FL; FL; AL; - ; June; Dysentery; Levy

POPE, Infant; 1; F; Black; FL; AL; AL; - ; June; Stillborn; Levy

CARTER, J; - ; F; M; FL; FL; FL; - ; June; Stillborn; Levy

CARLEY, J; - ; M; White; Ireland; Ireland; Ireland; Machinist;
Nov; Typhoid Fever; Levy

WASHINGTON, A; 25; M; Black; SC; SC; SC; Laborer; Mar;
Inflam/bowels; Levy

McILWANE, W.; 34; M; White; NC; DE; KY; Ship Mach.; July;
Accident; Levy

CANOVA, S; 26; M; White; SC; SC; SC; Laborer; Jan; Dropsey;
Levy

HAVEN, S; 54; F; White; SC; SC; SC; - ; Feb; Liver Complaint;
Levy

WALLER, Infant; 1; F; Black; FL; FL; FL; - ; June; Lung
Disease; Levy

Name; Age; Sex; Race; Born; FABorn; MOBorn;
          Occup; DODeath; Cause Of Death; County

TOOKE, J. B.; 34; M; White; FL; FL; FL; Fisherman; April;
    Consumption; Levy
WILSON, John; 55; M; - ; AL; AL; AL; Ship maker; Mar; Liver
    Complaint; Levy
STEVENS, S; - ; F; White; - ; - ; - ; - ; Feb; Fever; Levy
HOGANS, L. J.; 46; M; White; FL; GA; GA; Farmer; Aug;
    Dyspepsia; Levy
WYNN, Wm. H.; 69; M; White; GA; GA; GA; Farmer; July; - ;
    Levy
HARDEE, Tammy; 25; F; White; FL; GA; GA; - ; Sept; Cong.
    Chills; Levy
TILLIS, Julia A; 2; F; White; FL; GA; FL; - ; Oct; Brain Fever;
    Levy
TYNER, Susan; 68; F; White; SC; SC; SC; Farmer; Mar;
    Dysentery; Levy
STEPHENS, Ora; 1; F; White; FL; FL; FL; - ; Aug; Diarrhea;
    Levy
HENDRICKS, Daniel; 3; M; White; FL; AL; FL; - ; Feb; Fire;
    Levy
TYNER, Ailcey M.; 39; F; White; AL; SC; AL; - ; Nov; Dropsey;
    Levy
DENNIS, Ellen; 9; F; Black; FL; GA; GA; - ; April; Malarial
    Fever; Levy
DENNIS, Malvina; 11; F; Black; FL; GA; GA; - ; Feb; Typhoid
    Fever; Levy
LEWIS, Hattie; 15; F; Black; FL; GA; GA; - ; Sept; - ; Levy
GORE, Wm.; 72; M ; White; NC; NC; NC; ; Jan; - ; Levy
WASHINGTON, ORREN; 61; M; White; SC; - ; - ; Farmer; Dec;
    Consumption; Levy
B[unreadable], Pannley Ann; 33; F; White; FL; NC; NC; - ; Aug; -
    ; Levy
DUGGAN, Eli; 18; M; White; FL; GA; SC; Farmer; June; - ;
    Liberty
EASON, Bing; 11; M; White; FL; SC; GA; - ; Dec; Malarial
    Fever; Liberty
OXENDINE, Henry; 29; M; White; NC; NC; NC; Turpentine;
    June; Fell from horse; Liberty

TEDDIE, Estelle; 2; F; M; FL; GA; FL; - ; July; Ulcer head;
Liberty

BOYKIN, Rhoda; 1; F; White; FL; FL; FL; - ; Aug; Fever; Liberty

SPEIGHTS, Wm.; 66; M; White; GA; GA; GA; Carpenter; Mar;
Pneumonia; Liberty

PHILIPS, U. L.; 1; M; White; FL; GA; FL; - ; Aug; Whooping
cough; Liberty

FLOYD, Martha; 84; F; White; GA; GA; GA; - ; Oct; Palsey;
Liberty

RAMSEY, J. M.; 25; M; White; FL; GA; GA; Farmer; Mar;
Pneumonia; Liberty

PROCTOR, Ireney; 53; F; White; GA; GA; GA; Laborer; Jan;
Bright's Disease; Liberty

COLE, C. V.; 76; M; White; NY; NY; NY; Miller; Dec; Paralysis;
Liberty

TYNNER, [unreadable]; 31; M; White; FL; GA; FL; Farmer; Mar;
Cancer; Liberty

TURNER, M. T.; 26; M; White; FL; GA; FA; Laborer; Jan;
Typhoid Fever; Liberty

BATEMAN, R. R.; 30; M; White; FL; SC; SC; Merchant; Oct;
Pneumonia; Liberty

CHARLES, Jms.; 50; M; White; FL; SC; SC; Laborer; Dec; - ;
Liberty

BOYKIN, Reddie; 30; M; White; FL; GA; GA; Farmer; Mar;
Pneumonia; Liberty

WILLIAMS, E.; 1; F; Black; FL; FL; FL; - ; June; Consumption;
Madison

WILLIAMS, E.; 1; F; Black; FL; FL; FL; - ; Dec; Consumption;
Madison

MORROW, M.; 6; F; White; FL; SC; FL; - ; May; Consumption;
Madison

MORROW, W.; 11; M; White; FL; SC; FL; - ; May; Dysentery;
Madison

HIMOL, H.; 2; M; Black; FL; SC; SC; - ; Nov; Congestion;
Madison

LAW, Patty; 100; F; Black; FL; SC; SC; Farmer; Jan; Pneumonia;
Madison

Name; Age; Sex; Race; Born; FABorn; MOBorn;
        Occup; DODeath; Cause Of Death; County

WILSON, Phoebe; 75; F; Black; FL; SC; SC; Farmer; Feb;
    Jaundice; Madison
BROWN, Reuben; 50; M; White; SC; SC; SC; Farmer; Feb;
    Gastritis; Madison
PONDER, Mary; 10; F; Black; FL; FL; SC; Farmer; Feb;
    Dropsey; Madison
BRIDGES, B. F.; 4; m; White; FL; AL; FL; - ; Feb; Fire; Madison
LEE, Pearl; 2; F; Black; FL; FL; FL; - ; May; - ; Madison
WEAVER, John; 70; M; White; GA; - ; - ; Farmer; Mar; - ;
    Madison
WEAVER, Sarah; 36; F; White; GA; - ; - ; - ; Mar; - ; Madison
BROWN, Mary; 26; F; White; FL; FL; GA; - ; April; Dropsey;
    Madison
PLATT, Susan; 1; F; White; FL; Fl; FL; - ; Aug; Fever; Madison
NEWMAN, Ollie; 7; F; White; FL; SC; GA; - ; Nov; Bloody
    Fluid; Madison
HAYS, Wm. R.; 72; M; White; SC; Ireland; Ireland; Farmer; Nov;
    Paralysis; Madison
LAMM[?], Freonia; 27; F; White; GA; GA; GA; - ; Feb;
    Pneumonia; Madison
SINGLETON, Chas.; 23; M; Black; FL; SC; SC; Farmer; May;
    Pistol Ball; Madison
MARTIN, Flora; 24; F; Black; SC; SC; SC; Farmer; Dec;
    Dropsey; Madison
AGNEW, J. C.; 2; M; White; FL; - ; - ; - ; Jan; Cold; Madison
RICHERSON, D.; 57; M; White; GA; GA; GA; Farmer; April;
    Pneumonia; Madison
RICHERSON, F. J.; 29; M; White; FL; GA; GA; Farmer; Mar;
    Pneumonia; Madison
GENERAL, Louisa; 24; F; Black; FL; SC; TN; Farm; May;
    Confinement; Madison
WILLIAMS, Baby; 1; F; White; FL; AL; AL; - ; Aug; Dysentery;
    Madison
JONES, Emma J.; 16; F; White; FL; FL; FL; - ; Sept; Typhoid
    Fever; Madison
JOHNSON, Baby; 1; M; White; FL; GA; FL; - ; Sept; Over heat;
    Madison

SULLIVAN, Jon. S.; 1; M; White; FL; FL; FL; - ; May; Hives;
Madison
McCOLLOUGH, J. C.; 13; F; White; FL; FL; FL; - ; Oct; Cong.
Of Brain; Madison
DUCKWORTH, Rosa; 1; F; White; FL; SC; GA; - ; May;
Inflam/bowels; Madison
DUCKWORTH, J. F.; 1; M; White; FL; GA; FL; - ; Jan;
Pneumonia; Madison
SUTTON, C.; 20; F; Black; GA; GA; FL; Farming; Nov; Chills &
Fever; Madison
MITCHELL, Baby; 1; M; Black; FL; SC; SC; - ; Aug; - ; Madison
WHITE, M. J.; 11; F; White; FL; VA; FL; - ; Dec; Typhoid Fever;
Madison
WHITE, J. H.; 13; F; White; FL; VA; FL; - ; Jan; Typhoid Fever;
Madison
HALL, Nettie; 20; F; Black; FL; SC; GA; Laborer; May; Child
Birth; Madison
GARRETT, Gus; 16; M; Black; FL; SC; - ; Laborer; Nov;
Pneumonia; Madison
HILL, John; 19; M; Black; FL; SC; - ; Laborer; Sept; Bilious
Fever; Madison
HILL, Trey; 3; F; Black; FL; - ; SC; - ; May; Dropsey; Madison
SMITH, Ge[?]; 1; M; Black; FL; GA; FL; - ; Sept; Born dead;
Madison
DASHER, Benj.; 40; M; Black; SC; SC; SC; Laborer; May;
Dropsey; Madison
JONES, C. J.; 2; M; Black; FL; FL; FL; - ; Sept; Dysentery;
Madison
EARLE, Sis; 1; F; Black; FL; FL; FL; - ; Feb; Hives; Madison
MARTIE, Hilon; 2; F; Black; FL; FL; FL; - ; June; Fever;
Madison
ARMSTEAD, Wm.; 38; M; Black; GA; GA; GA; Farmer; Nov;
Killed in jail; Madison
SIMMONS, Maggie; 1; F; Black; FL; FL; FL; - ; Jan; Teething;
Madison
HILL, Wilmer F.; 21; M; White; AL; AL; AL; Teacher; Feb;
Typhoid Fever; Madison

Name; Age; Sex; Race; Born; FABorn; MOBorn;
        Occup; DODeath; Cause Of Death; County

TUCKER, Peter; 4; M; Black; GA; GA; GA; - ; Aug; Fever;
    Madison
TUCKER, Millard; 2; M; Black; GA; GA; GA; - ; Nov; Fever;
    Madison
CAMPBELL, Geo.; 5; M; Black; FL; GA; GA; - ; Feb; Diptheria;
    Madison
WHARTIN, Ella; 40; F; White; VA; VA; VA; Housewife; Jan;
    Cancer/stomach; Madison
PEACOCK, Ferrell; 1; M; Black; FL; NC; SC; - ; May; Cholera
    Infection; Madison
PEACOC, Moses ; 1; M; Black; FL; NC; SC; - ; Aug; Cholera
    Infection; Madison
HART, John; 79; M; White; SC; SC; SC; Merchant; June;
    Typhoid Fever; Madison
BRINSON, Ann; 53; F; White; FL; FL; FL; Housekeep; June;
    Consumption; Madison
THOMAS, Laura L.; 36; F; White; FL; SC; GA; Housewife; Sept;
    Congestion; Madison
BRINSON, Mary; 30; F; White; FL; GA; GA; - ; Feb;
    Inflam/bowels; Madison
THOMAS, Mary L.; 14; F; White; FL; FL; FL; - ; June; Typhoid
    Fever; Madison
DICKINSON, Fredonia; 27; F; White; FL; GA; GA; Housewife;
    June; Typhoid Fever; Madison
McLEARY, Maggie; 28; F; White; FL; NC; NC; - ; Aug;
    Hemmorrhage; Madison
LIVINGSTON, S. H.; 1; F; White; FL; SC; GA; - ; Dec; Cholera
    Infection; Madison
STREETY, T. J.; 1; M; White; FL; FL; FL; - ; Oct; Cholera
    Infection; Madison
ROLAND, Robt. C.; 1; M; White; FL; FL; FL; - ; June;
    Cong/lungs; Madison
SMITH, S. H.; 48; F; White; GA; RI; RI; Housewife; May;
    Cong/bowels; Madison
JOHNSON, Saml.; 15; M; White; FL; FL; FL; - ; Feb; Shot &
    killed; Madison
McCAMMA, Rebecca; 65; F; White; GA; GA; GA; - ; Aug; Heart
    Disease; Madison

DANIEL, Robt.; 60; M; White; GA; GA; GA; Porter; Mar; Heart
Disease; Madison
HORRELL, Eddy; 4; F; White; FL; FL; FL; - ; Aug; Congestion;
Madison
HORRELL, Shelby; 1; F; White; FL; FL; FL; - ; Dec; Congestion;
Madison
POUND, Ashby; 1; M; White; GA; GA; MS; - ; Oct; Congestion;
Madison
DEAN, John; 80; M; White; FL; FL; GA; Farmer; May;
Pneumonia; Madison
KIRBY, Eliza; 80; F; White; SC; SC; SC; - ; June; Pneumonia;
Madison
MATHERS, Elijah; 24; M; Black; FL; VA; VA; Mill hand; Feb;
Drowned; Madison
SMITH, Nellie; 25; F; Black; FL; FL; GA; Cook; Aug; Fever;
Madison
WEBB, Ella; 1; F; White; FL; FL; GA; - ; April; Inflam/bowels;
Madison
WHEELER, Thomas; 1; M; Black; FL; FL; FL; - ; Feb; Cholera
Infection; Madison
SMITH, Mary F.; 30; F; White; NY; NY; NY; - ; Sept;
Pneumonia; Madison
NEBRASKA, Mitchell; 2; M; White; FL; FL; GA; - ; Mar;
Inflam/bowels; Madison
BELLOWS, Thos. B; 78; M; White; NY; NY; NY; Mechanic; Jan;
Neuro Disability; Madison
ANDREWS, Jms.; 40; M; White; FL; FL; FL; Mechanic; May;
Pneumonia; Madison
LEE, Eliza; 35; F; White; FL; FL; FL; Cook; June; Pneumonia;
Madison
ADAMS, Jane; 1; F; White; FL; FL; FL; - ; Oct; Cholera
Infection; Madison
BLOCKER, Jeffrey; 4; M; Black; FL; FL; SC; - ; Oct; Fever;
Madison
HARRELL, James; 1; M; Black; FL; FL; SC; - ; May; Cholera
Infection; Madison
MUNROE, Thomas; 30; M; Black; FL; FL; SC; Blacksmith; Dec;
Explosion; Madison

64   Name; Age; Sex; Race; Born; FABorn; MOBorn;
         Occup; DODeath; Cause Of Death; County

DOUGLASS, John; 23; M; Black; FL; FL; SC; Boat Hand; June;
     Gravel; Madison
DOUGLASS, Nelly; 2; F; Black; FL; FL; SC; - ; Aug; Teething;
     Madison
SMITH, Mary; 30; F; White; NY; NY; NY; - ; Sept; Pneumonia;
     Madison
MOORE, Jerry; 8; M; Black; FL; FL; FL; - ; Sept; Fever; Madison
BLAKE, F. B.; 14; M; White; FL; FL; FL; - ; May; Heart
     Malformation Madison;
BLAKE, H. L.; 18; F; White; FL; FL; FL; - ; Oct; Typhoid Fever;
     Madison
BLAKE, I. I.; 23; M; White; FL; FL; FL; - ; May; Dropsey;
     Madison
WALKER, John; 9; M; Black; FL; FL; FL; - ; June; Fever;
     Madison
WALKER, Benj.; 7; M; Black; FL; FL; FL; - ; June; Fever;
     Madison
WALKER, Arthur; 5; M; Black; FL; FL; FL; - ; June; Worms;
     Madison
JONES, Lilla; 9; F; Black; FL; GA; FL; - ; May; Worms/Fever;
     Madison
AMBROSE, Howard; 8; M; Black; FL; SC; FL; - ; April;
     Dropsey; Madison
DICE, Emery; 4; M; White; FL; Fl; FL; - ; June; Congestion
     Brain; Madison
MYRRICK, Infant; 1; F; White; FL; FL; FL; - ; Oct; Premature
     birth; Madison
JONES, Lovet; 5; M; Black; FL; GA; FL; - ; June; Intestinal
     worms; Madison
HAYRICK, Gulleye; 18; F; White; FL; SC; FL; Farming; Sept;
     Child bed fever; Madison
JOHNSON, Martha; 50; F; White; SC; SC; SC; - ; April; Bilious
     Fever; Madison
JONES, Edward; 80; M; Black; MD; MD; MD; Blacksmith; June;
     Old Age; Madison
MARSHAL, Lottie; 2; F; Black; FL; - ; - ; - ; Sept; Worms;
     Madison

MARSHAL, Elizabeth; 30; F; Black; FL; SC; SC; Cook; Dec;
Consumption; Madison
SMITH, Ritta; 20; F; Black; FL; SC; SC; Laborer; - ; Siphilis;
Madison
DELAUGHTER, Frances; 45; F; Black; SC; SC; SC; Laborer; - ;
Congestive fever; Madison
PINKNEY, Newsom; 1; M; Black; FL; FL; FL; - ; Aug; Teething;
Madison
TUTEN, Mary H.; 54; F; White; GA; SC; SC; Farming; Dec;
Typhoid Fever; Madison
STEPHENS, Dan'l.; 70; M; Black; GA; GA; GA; Farming; Aug;
Congestive fever; Madison
HARWELL, Miles; 40; M; White; GA; GA; GA; Farming; Aug;
Dropsey; Madison
HARWELL, Laura; 10; F; White; FL; GA; GA; - ; May; Dropsey;
Madison
ARNOLD, Mary; 30; F; White; GA; GA; GA; Domestic; - ;
Childbed Fever; Madison
ARNOLD, Infant; 1; F; White; FL; GA; GA; - ; - ; Premature
birth; Madison
MONTGOMERY, M. E.; 76; M; White; SC; Ireland; Ireland;
Farming; Oct; Pneumonia; Madison
MONTGOMERY, M. J. S.; 74; F; White; SC; SC; SC; Housewife;
Nov; Dropsey; Madison
SMITH, S. R.; 53; M; White; GA; SC; SC; Farming; July; Bilious
Fever; Madison
HUMPHREY, Esther; 22; F; Black; FL; NC; SC; Housework; Jan;
Consumption; Madison
HUMPHREY, Anne; 1; F; Black; FL; FL; FL; - ; Nov; Hives;
Madison
HUMPHREY, Chester; 3; M; Black; FL; FL; FL; - ; Jan;
Consumption; Madison
McENTYRE, Stella; 2; F; White; FL; AL; FL; - ; July;
Cong/Brain; Madison
MANUEL, Isaac; 70; M; Black; VA; VA; VA; Farming; July;
Asthma; Madison
L[unreadable], Baby; 1; F; M; FL; GA; SC; - ; April; Born dead;
Madison

GUNN, Manuel; 75; M; Black; VA; Africa; VA; Farm hand; Feb;
   Piles & gravel; Madison
MARTIN, Chas.; 11; M; White; GA; GA; GA; Farm hand; - ;
   Pneumonia; Madison
SIMMONS, Baby; 1; M; White; FL; - ; - ; - ; Mar; Born dead;
   Madison
BEATY, H. D.; 68; M; White; GA; Ireland; GA; Farming; Sept;
   Pneumonia; Madison
CARES (?), Wm; 23; M; White; FL; SC; SC; - ; Nov; Epilepsy;
   Madison
ETHERIDGE, Jno.; 48; M; White; AL; AL; AL; Farming; May;
   Paralysis; Madison
OWENS, Elizabeth; 61; F; White; SC; SC; SC; Farmer; June;
   Dropsey; Madison
DUVAL, Sallie; 7; F; White; FL; VA; FL; - ; Dec; Cong./Brain;
   Madison
CARRAWAY, H. M.; 26; M; White; FL; SC; SC; Farmer; Jan;
   Bilious Fever; Madison
COOK, Mollie; 1; F; White; FL; FL; FL; - ; Oct; Pneumonia;
   Madison
TOWNSEND, Sarah; 85; F; White; SC; SC; SC; - ; Feb; Old Age;
   Madison
CASON, Wallace; 1; M; Black; FL; FL; FL; - ; Sept; Fever;
   Madison
COFFEE, Mary; 11; F; Black; FL; GA; GA; - ; July; Bilious
   Fever; Madison
COFFEE, Julia; 8; F; Black; FL; GA; GA; - ; May; Bilious Fever;
   Madison
COFFEE, Wiley; 62; M; M; GA; GA; GA; Farmer; Dec; Old Age;
   Madison
BARRETT, Henry; 17; M; White; FL; FL; FL; - ; Mar; Dropsey;
   Madison
WARNOCK, Lawton; 38; M; White; FL; FL; FL; Farmer; April;
   Abcess/liver; Madison
LANGFORD, G. W.; 27; M; White; FL; GA; GA; Farmer; May;
   Shot & killed; Madison
MOODY, JR., Bob; 5; M; White; FL; GA; FL; - ; Feb;
   Pneumonia; Madison

COX, Mary; 23; F; White; FL; FL; AL; - ; - ; Measles; Madison
ELMORE, Ed; 40; M; Black; FL; FL; FL; - ; July; Leprosy;
Madison
LESLIE, Sue; 1; F; White; FL; FL; FL; - ; May; Dysentery;
Madison
PHILLIPS, Emeline; 37; F; White; SC; SC; SC; Farmer; June;
Confinement; Madison
HARRIS, Jno.; 4; M; Black; FL; FL; FL; - ; June; Worms;
Madison
HARRIS, Hadley; 12; M; Black; FL; FL; FL; - ; Jan; Worms;
Madison
TRUMAN, Florida; 1; F; Black; FL; FL; FL; - ; June; Unknown;
Madison
TOOKE, Caro; 3; F; Black; GA; FL; GA; - ; Sept; Dropsey;
Madison
TOOKE, Lotty; 1; F; Black; GA; FL; GA; - ; Sept; Scarlet Fever;
Madison
SMITH, Sylvestia; 60; F; Black; VA; VA; VA; Housekeep; Feb;
Unknown; Madison
MONROE, Abe; 60; M; Black; FL; FL; FL; Blacksmith; Nov;
Paralysis; Madison
ROUNTREE, Chas.; 13; M; Black; FL; GA; FL; - ; Mar;
Epilepsy; Madison
STUBBS, Jos.; 5; M; White; FL; SC; FL; - ; Dec; Hematoma;
Madison
SCOTT, Mitchell; 16; M; White; FL; GA; SC; - ; Feb; Eating Dirt;
Madison
LONG, Willie; 16; M; Black; FL; GA; GA; - ; Oct; Poison;
Madison
WILLIAMS, Tim; 10; M; Black; FL; FL; FL; - ; April; Unknown;
Madison
WILLIAMS, Ed; 5; M; Black; FL; Fl; SC; - ; Oct; Bleeding navel;
Madison
WILLIAMS, Mary; 1; F; Black; FL; FL; SC; - ; June; Unknown;
Madison
WILLIAMS, Martha; 1; F; Black; FL; FL; SC; - ; June; Unknown;
Madison

Name; Age; Sex; Race; Born; FABorn; MOBorn;
        Occup; DODeath; Cause Of Death; County

PANDY, Fanny; 46; F; M; GA; - ; GA; Housekeep; June; Asthma;
    Madison
BARCLAY, E. P.; 20; M; White; FL; GA; GA; Farmer; Aug;
    Cong.Brain; Madison
HAMPTON, E. T.; 8; M; White; FL; GA; GA; - ; Aug;
    Cong.Brain/bowels; Madison
BRICKHAMMER, Mary; 1; F; M; FL; FL; FL; - ; Dec; Cong.
    Bowels; Madison
MCINTIRE, Dilsey; 6; F; Black; FL; FL; FL; - ; Aug; Worms;
    Madison
BEMIS, Louisa; 66; F; White; MA; MA; MA; Housekeep; Oct;
    Consumption; Madison
HARRISON, Kitty; 76; F; Black; FL; FL; FL; Farm Labor; Oct;
    Unknown; Madison
YOUNG, Margaret; 10; F; Black; FL; SC; SC; - ; June; Heart
    Pain; Madison
CLEMENS, Dolls; 5; M; Black; FL; SC; SC; - ; June; Jaundice;
    Madison
STEWARD, Abby; 80; F; Black; VA; LA; LA; Cook; April;
    Dropsey; Madison
DAVIS, Cornelius; 1; M; Black; FL; SC; SC; - ; Aug; Croup;
    Madison
HINES, H. B.; 1; M; White; FL; GA; FL; - ; Jan; - ; Madison
HINES, Geo. Thos. ; 3; M; White; FL; GA; FL; - ; Sept;
    Cong.Brain; Madison
WHITE, Matthew; 35; M; Black; FL; - ; - ; Farmer; Feb;
    Consumption; Madison
RADFORD, Scott; 38; M; White; GA; GA; NC; Farmer; April;
    Suicide; Madison
WHITE, Jeanie; 70; F; Black; SC; - ; - ; - ; Jan; Asthma; Madison
WHITE, Madison; 35; M; Black; FL; SC; SC; Farmer; Feb;
    Consumption; Madison
ADAMS, Louisa; 40; F; Black; NC; NC; NC; Housekeep; May;
    Stomach Pain; Madison
LEE, Lizzie; 23; F; White; FL; SC; NC; Laborer; Mar; Typhoid
    Fever; Madison
LIVINGSTON, Tom; 2; M; Black; FL; FL; FL; - ; Aug; Worms;
    Madison

HALL, Patty; 3; F; Black; FL; GA; FL; - ; Mar; Typhoid Fever;
Madison

KERSEY, Elizabeth; 45; F; White; FL; GA; GA; Housekeep;
April; Typhoid Fever; Madison

CALLAHAN, James; 48; M; White; GA; GA; GA; Farmer; May;
Brain/Heart Pain; Madison

HENRY, Geo.; 72; M; Black; SC; VA; VA; Blacksmith; Sept;
Gravel; Madison

MILLER, Chas.; 1; M; Black; FL; NC; SC; - ; May; Whooping
cough; Madison

JOHNSON, Fleming; 37; M; M; FL; SC; SC; Farmer; April; Gun
Shot; Madison

JOHNSON, Lizzie; 7; F; - ; FL; FL; FL; - ; Oct; Fever; Madison

JOHNSON, Ladie; 75; F; Black; AL; AL; AL; - ; April; Asthma;
Madison

GAMBLE, Rose; 21; F; Black; FL; SC; SC; Laborer; April;
Dropsey; Madison

GAMBLE, Margaret; 1; F; Black; FL; SC; FL; - ; May; Cholera
Infection; Madison

GLEE, Shellie; 9; F; Black; FL; FL; FL; - ; May; Cholera
Infection; Madison

ASHLEY, Jos.; 1; M; Black; FL; FL; FL; - ; Oct; Teething;
Madison

RUTHERFORD, Sila; 20; F; White; FL; SC; SC; - ; Aug; Cong.
Chills; Madison

GRIFFIN, Solomon; 3; M; Black; FL; FL; FL; - ; Feb; Worms;
Madison

DAVIS, Robt.; 2; M; Black; FL; FL; FL; - ; May; Dysentery;
Madison

COFFEE, Sallie; 1; F; M; FL; FL; FL; - ; Sept; Fever; Madison

WARREN, Virginia; 36; F; M; SC; SC; SC; Laborer; May;
Pneumonia; Madison

MILLER, Jno.; 70; M; Black; SC; SC; SC; - ; June; - ; Madison

JONES, Anna; 23; M; Black; FL; FL; VA; Laborer; Mar;
Dropsey; Madison

USHER, Hezekiah; 3; M; M; FL; NC; SC; - ; Aug; Fever;
Madison

Name; Age; Sex; Race; Born; FABorn; MOBorn;
        Occup; DODeath; Cause Of Death; County

ALEXANDER, S[?]; 7; F; Black; FL; SC; - ; - ; July; Bowel
    Disease; Madison
MITCHELL, Chas.; 75; M; Black; SC; SC; SC; - ; Jan;
    Pneumonia; Madison
MITCHELL, Kitty; 55; F; Black; SC; SC; SC; - ; Feb; Pneumonia;
    Madison
JOHNSON, Brutus; 36; M; M; FL; SC; SC; - ; July; Consumption;
    Madison
JONES, Minnie; 2; F; Black; FL; FL; FL; - ; April; Consumption;
    Madison
MONROE, Abram; 45; M; Black; FL; SC; SC; Blacksmith; Dec;
    Pneumonia; Madison
MCKINNEY, Olive; 17; F; Black; FL; GA; GA; Laborer; Sept;
    Consumption; Madison
MCKINNEY, Jacob; 65; M; Black; GA; GA; GA; Carpenter; Mar;
    Paralysis; Madison
RICHARDSON, Wm.; 80; M; M; SC; SC; SC; Farmer; Oct;
    Consumption; Madison
GLASS, J. F.; 55; M; White; VA; VA; VA; Farmer; Mar;
    Pneumonia; Madison
COFFEE, Lancaster; 23; M; M; FL; FL; FL; Farmer; July; Bilious
    Fever; Madison
DIXON, Rosa; 1; F; Black; FL; SC; SC; - ; April; Dysentery;
    Madison
DIXON, Ben; 1; M; Black; FL; SC; MS; - ; April; Brain Fever;
    Madison
SLOAN, Emma; 10; F; M; FL; MS; NC; - ; Oct; Fever; Madison
JONES, Millie; 37; F; M; FL; NC; NC; Laborer; Sept; Typhoid
    Fever; Madison
WHITEHURST, Sentia; 60; F; Black; VA; VA; VA; - ; Jan;
    Pneumonia; Madison
COLLIER, Sophie; 50; F; Black; GA; GA; GA; Laborer; Feb;
    Pneumonia; Madison
SHAW, Elder; 1; M; Black; FL; SC; SC; - ; Aug; Fever; Madison
GHENT, Elizabeth; 2; M; Black; FL; FL; FL; - ; July; Worms;
    Madison
P[?], Sophie; 25; F; Black; GA; GA; GA; Laborer; Oct; - ;
    Madison

CARLTON, Florence; 14; F; White; FL; - ; - ; - ; June; Heart
Disease; Manatee

HENDRY, Emma; 35; F; Black; FL; - ; - ; - ; Aug; Acc. Gun shot;
Manatee

PARKER, Hooker; 2; M; White; FL; FL; FL; - ; Mar;
Complications; Manatee

HERNDON, Mrs.; 73; F; White; GA; GA; GA; - ; June; Dropsey;
Manatee

HANCOCK, Mrs.; 43; F; White; - ; - ; - ; - ; May; Confinement;
Manatee

WILSON, Mr.; 30; M; White; FL; - ; - ; - ; Dec; Malarial Fever;
Manatee

MERCER, Julia; 21; F; White; FL; GA; GA; - ; Feb;
Complications; Manatee

NORTH, John; 50; F; White; GA; GA; GA; - ; May; Congestion;
Manatee

NORTH, Rebecca; 18; F; White; FA; GA; GA; - ; April;
Confinement; Manatee

ALDERMAN, Liman; 3; M; White; FL; FL; FL; - ; Nov;
Congestion; Manatee

WILKINS, N. A.; 3; F; White; FL; AL; GA; - ; Oct; Inflam/liver;
Manatee

GILL, Martha Jane; 8; F; White; FL; FL; GA; - ; May; Fever;
Manatee

CARLTON, Mable; 3; F; White; FL; FL; FL; - ; Dec; Fever;
Manatee

ALBRITTON, James; 66; M; White; GA; - ; - ; Farmer; Nov;
Dropsey; Manatee

CREWS, Mary; - ; F; White; - ; - ; - ; - ; - ; Heart Disease;
Manatee

HUNTER, E.; - ; F; White; GA; GA; GA; - ; July; Comsumption;
Manatee

B[unreadable],; - ; F; White; FL; GA; GA; - ; Aug; Dropsey;
Manatee

WHIDDON, Arilla; 4; F; White; FL; GA; GA; - ; - ; Bilious
Fever; Manatee

HART, James; 6; M; White; FL; GA; GA; - ; May; Cholera
Infection; Manatee

Name; Age; Sex; Race; Born; FABorn; MOBorn;
Occup; DODeath; Cause Of Death; County

MINYELL(?), Jesse B; 33; M; White; FL; GA; GA; Farmer; June;
Shot/by F.M.Platt; Manatee

MORY, N. W.; 1; F; White; FL; FL; FL; - ; June; Pleurisy of
head; Manatee

WILSON, George; 5; M; Black; SC; SC; SC; - ; July ; Croup;
Marion

MICLE (MICHAEL), Jacob; 11; M; Black; FL; FL; FL; - ; Dec;
Typhoid Fever; Marion

DAVIS, Anna; 1; F; Black; FL; NC; FL; - ; Aug; Premature birth;
Marion

WARD, Henrietta; 9; F; Black; FL; SC; SC; - ; Jan; Colic; Marion

YOUNG, Lucy; 3; F; White; FL; FL; FL; - ; Oct;
Congestion/liver; Marion

THOMAS, Jessie; 1; F; Black; FL; FL; FL; - ; Sept; Thrash;
Marion

MATHEWS, JR., Geo. G.; 8; M; White; Brazil; AL; AL; - ; June;
Measles; Marion

WARD, Laura M; 58; F; Black; GA; GA; GA; Housekeep; April;
Dysentery; Marion

SMALL, Saml.; 6; M; Black; FL; SC; SC; - ; Sept; Dysentery;
Marion

AUSTIN, Kate; 53; F; Black; GA; GA; GA; Housekeep; Dec;
Paralysis; Marion

DUPUIS, D. S.; 69; M; White; SC; SC; SC; Farmer; May;
Paralysis; Marion

TAYLOR, Rebecca; 28; F; Black; SC; SC; SC; - ; Dec; Child Bed;
Marion

TAYLOR, Infant; 1; M; Black; FL; SC; SC; - ; Dec; Stillborn;
Marion

APPLEBY, Ella E.; 14; F; White; SC; SC; SC; - ; May; Bilious
Fever; Marion

DAWSEY, Mollie; 1; F; Black; FL; FL; SC; - ; June; Measles;
Marion

SMITH, Marshal; 3; M; White; FL; FL; SC; - ; Nov; Cong. brain;
Marion

HAMON, Peter; 40; M; Black; SC; SC; SC; Farmer; June;
Pneumonia; Marion

WASHINGTON, Mary; 15; F; Black; FL; SC; SC; - ; May;
Dropsey; Marion

JENKINS, Mary; 86; F; M; SC; SC; SC; Housekeep; Sept; Bilious
Fever; Marion

JENKINS, Hannah; 56; F; M; SC; SC; SC; Housekeep; Aug; Hurt;
Marion

STEPHENS, A. M.; 35; M; White; KY; KY; KY; Lawyer; Mar;
Spinal Fever; Marion

MARTIN, Gardner; 84; M; Black; GA; GA; GA; Farmer; Mar;
Pneumonia; Marion

BURLISON, Mary; 25; F; Black; FL; SC; SC; - ; May; Syphilus;
Marion

FLOYD, Amy; 24; F; Black; FL; SC; SC; Housekeep; Sept;
Consumption; Marion

JONES, Jannett; 40; F; Black; SC; SC; SC; Laborer; Mar;
Dropsey; Marion

JORDAN, Stephen; 70; M; Black; GA; GA; GA; Farmer; April;
Dropsey; Marion

RHODES, Geo. W.; 1; M; White; FL; FL; FL; - ; Mar; Diptheria;
Marion

BRUTON, Mamie; 11; F; White; FL; - ; GA; - ; Oct; Pneumonia;
Marion

NIEL, Mary; 1; F; White; FL; FL; GA; - ; April; Fever; Marion

HAGOOD, R. R. ; 73; M; White; VA; VA; VA; Farmer; Oct; Old
Age; Marion

LEITNER, M. H.; 39; F; White; GA; GA; GA; - ; Aug;
Consumption; Marion

GREENE, A; 65; M; Black; SC; SC; SC; Farmer; Feb; Fever;
Marion

LUFFMAN, N. T.; 17; M; White; FL; NC; NC; Farmer; Aug;
Fever; Marion

BOYT, R. R.; 12; F; White; FL; GA; FL; - ; April; Congestion;
Marion

WEATHERS, I.; 80; M; Black; SC; SC; SC; Farmer; Mar; Old
Age; Marion

BELL, Martha; 1; F; Black; FL; SC; SC; - ; May; Cong/bowels;
Marion

74   Name; Age; Sex; Race; Born; FABorn; MOBorn;
          Occup; DODeath; Cause Of Death; County

DUPREY, P. J.; 4; M; White; LA; LA; LA; - ; Nov; Bilious Fever;
    Marion
DUPREY, A.; 1; F; White; LA; LA; LA; - ; Sept; Gastritis;
    Marion
MAY, R; 29; M; Black; FL; SC; SC; Farmer; Nov; Fever; Marion
DAUGHTRY, M; 32; F; White; FL; GA; GA; - ; Mar; Comb. Of
    disease; Marion
DOYLE, I.; 65; M; Black; GA; GA; GA; Laborer; Mar; Scrofula;
    Marion
LINDER, L.; 6; F; Black; FL; SC; FL; - ; July; Cong/brain;
    Marion
MENCH, Annie Eliza; 21; F; White; Bahamas; Bahamas;
    Bahamas; - ; Feb; Periotinitis; Monroe
HERERA, Providencia; 1; F; White; Key West; Cuba; Cuba; - ;
    Feb; Convulsions; Monroe
GOIEN, Nancy E; 22; F; White; FL; FL; FL; - ; Feb; Typhoid
    Fever; Monroe
YATES, Sarah; 50; F; Black; Bahamas; Bahamas; Bahamas;
    Laborer; Feb; Convulsions; Monroe
BAKER, Benj.; 2; M; White; Key West; Key West; Key West; - ;
    Feb; Consumption; Monroe
VENTURA, Elias; 56; M; White; Cuba; Cuba; Cuba; Cigarmaker;
    Feb; Rheumatism; Monroe
CHAVEZ, Esteban; 32; M; White; Cuba; Cuba; Cuba;
    Cigarmaker; Feb; Plebitis; Monroe
ROSEN, J.; 22; M; Black; Bahamas; Bahamas; Bahamas; Seaman;
    Feb; Pulmanary; Monroe
CASEY, Char.; 1; M; White; Key West; Key West; Key West; - ;
    Feb; Cholera Infection; Monroe
MESENA, Cornelia; 28; F; White; Cuba; Cuba; Cuba; Laborer;
    Feb; Tuberculosis; Monroe
HENOSA, Clotilde; 20; F; Black; Cuba; Cuba; Cuba; Laborer;
    Feb; Tuberculosis; Monroe
SWEENY, Temple; 1; M; White; Key West; NJ; NY; - ; Feb;
    Cholera Infection; Monroe
WESSON, P. V.; 35; M; White; TN; TN; TN; Laborer; Feb;
    Phthisis; Monroe

SNIDER, David; 70; M; White; FL; NJ; NY; Laborer; Feb; Senile
Decay; Monroe
LAUNI, Ed. N.; 3; M; Black; Key West; - ; - ; - ; Feb;
Convulsions; Monroe
SANDERS, Sarah; 1; F; Black; Key West; - ; - ; - ; Feb; Defective
Vitality; Monroe
MARTINEZ, Guillermo; 1; M; White; Key West; Cuba; Cuba; - ;
Feb; Enteritis; Monroe
SANDERS, Wm.; 1; M; Black; Key West; - ; - ; - ; Feb; Defective
Vitality; Monroe
BETHEA, Marie; 2; F; Black; Key West; - ; - ; - ; Feb; Pertusis;
Monroe
LA HERNANDEZ, Antonio; 35; M; White; Havana; Cuba; Cuba;
Cigarmaker; Feb; Consumption; Monroe
JEFFREY, Benj.; 95; M; Black; VA; VA; VA; - ; Feb; Senile
Decay; Monroe
SINCLAIR, Jn.; 10; M; Black; Key West; Key West; Key West; -
; Feb; Peritonitis; Monroe
VANETA, Sofia; 1; F; White; Key West; - ; - ; - ; Feb; Cholera
Infection; Monroe
VON PFULER[?], Wm. H.; 75; M; White; SC; SC; SC; - ; Feb;
Angina; Monroe
BUNQUE, Jose; 30; M; Black; Cuba; Cuba; Cuba; Cigarmaker;
Feb; Pulmonary; Monroe
ZAMORA, Anselino; 1; M; White; Key West; Key West; Key
West; - ; Feb; Lung Disease; Monroe
JOSE, Julia; 1; F; Black; Key West; - ; - ; - ; Mar; Marasmus;
Monroe
ALFONSO, Henry; 1; M; White; Key West; - ; - ; - ; Mar;
Meningitis; Monroe
GUERIA, Anna C.; 1; F; White; Key West; Cuba; Cuba; - ; Mar;
Colitis; Monroe
FUENTES, Cecano; 1; M; Black; Key West; Cuba; Cuba; - ; Mar;
Colitis; Monroe
RAMIREZ, Justina; 1; F; White; Key West; Cuba; Cuba; - ; Mar;
Brain Fever; Monroe
PAREDA, Casimera; 1; M; Black; Key West; Cuba; Cuba; - ;
Mar; Lockjaw; Monroe

76   Name; Age; Sex; Race; Born; FABorn; MOBorn;
         Occup; DODeath; Cause Of Death; County

KNIGHT, Mary Babcock; 1; F; White; Key West; Key West; Key
    West; - ; Mar; Cholera Infection; Monroe
BETHEL, Olone; 21; F; Black; Key West; Bahamas; Bahamas; - ;
    Mar; Pertusis; Monroe
SPENCER, Lewis; 41; M; White; Bahamas; Bahamas; Bahamas;
    Cigarmaker; Mar; Cut throat; Monroe
PORTLOCK, Mary; 17; F; White; Key West; Bahamas; Bahamas;
    Laborer; Mar; Pulmonalsis; Monroe
ORICKE, Frederick; 1; M; White; Key West; Cuba; Cuba; - ; Dec;
    Convulsions; Monroe
SHAVER, Lucy; 29; F; Black; FL; FL; FL; - ; Dec; Bright's
    Disease; Monroe
CHAPURO, Jo.; 1; M; White; Key West; Cuba; Cuba; - ; Dec;
    Accident; Monroe
CAREDES, Juan; 1; M; Black; Key West; Cuba; Cuba; - ; Dec;
    Whooping cough; Monroe
SWEETING, Amelia; 1; F; White; Key West; Bahamas; Bahamas;
    - ; Dec; Inanition; Monroe
FONTANELLO, Mauna; 45; F; White; Cuba; Cuba; Cuba;
    Laborer; Dec; Cirrosis of Liver; Monroe
KNOWLES, Gilbert A.; 2; M; White; Key West; Bahamas;
    Bahamas; - ; Jan; Asthma; Monroe
WAGNER, Herman; 59; M; White; Germany; Germany;
    Germany; Seaman; Jan; Dysentery; Monroe
MORROW, Robert; 36; M; White; Bahamas; Bahamas; Bahamas;
    Seaman; Jan; Heart Disease; Monroe
PHILBROOKS, Richard A.; 1; M; Black; Key West; FL; FL; - ;
    Jan; Chronic Hydrocep.; Monroe
SAUNDERS, Felicia; 1; F; White; Key West; Bahamas; Bahamas;
    - ; Jan; Fever; Monroe
COLEBROOK, Frank; 80; M; Black; Africa; Africa; Africa;
    Laborer; Jan; Dysentery; Monroe
KELLY, Ann; 13; F; Black; Bahamas; Bahamas; Bahamas; - ; Jan;
    Pertusis; Monroe
GOMEZ, Francisco; 2; M; White; Key West; Cuba; Cuba; - ; Jan;
    Fever; Monroe
MORRIS, Edw.; 24; M; Black; Bahamas; Bahamas; Bahamas;
    Laborer; Jan; Phthisis; Monroe

RUIS, Antonio; 1; M; Black; Key West; Cuba; Cuba; - ; July;
[unreadable]; Monroe

CAMY[?], Ellen; 3; F; White; Key West; Bahamas; Bahamas; - ;
July; Whooping cough; Monroe

YEATES, Mattie; 1; F; Black; Key West; Bahamas; Bahamas; - ;
Juy; - ; Monroe

PELFORI, Matilda; 34; F; White; Cuba; Cuba; Cuba; - ; July;
Typhoid Fever; Monroe

PINDER, Cora B.; 1; F; White; Key West; Key West; Key West; -
; July; Consumption; Monroe

CARY, Infant; 1; F; White; Key West; Bahamas; Bahamas; - ;
July; Consumption; Monroe

VIALEH, Felix; 1; M; Black; Key West; Cuba; Cuba; ; July;
Cong. Brain; Monroe

ASHLEY, Pricilla C.; 15; F; Black; Bahamas; Bahamas; Bahamas;
Maid; July; Cong. Brain; Monroe

THRIFT, Emma; 88; F; White; Bahamas; Bahamas; Bahamas; - ;
July; Intestinal Obstruc.; Monroe

GONZALEZ, Manuel; 1; M; White; Key West; Cuba; Cuba;
Carpenter; July; Cancer; Monroe

CUNNINGHAM, Jazz; 49; M; Black; Bahamas; Bahamas;
Bahamas; - ; July; Consumption; Monroe

BROCKWAY, Lewis; 11; M; Black; Key West; USA; USA; - ;
July; Typhoid Fever; Monroe

INGRAHAM, Infant; 1; M; White; Key West; Bahamas;
Bahamas; - ; July; [unreadable]; Monroe

MARTINBURG, Susan E.; 1; F ; Black; Key West; Africa;
Africa; - ; July; [unreadable]; Monroe

ACOSTA, Alphonse A.; 1; M; M; Key West; Cuba; Cuba; - ; July;
Cholera Infection; Monroe

CASTRO, Filipe; 1; M; White; Key West; Spain; Spain; - ; July;
Consumption; Monroe

KNOWLES, Thomas; 1; M; White; Key West; USA; USA; - ;
July; Thrash; Monroe

BETANCOURT, Mercedes; 22; F; White; Cuba; Spain; Spain;
Tobacco St.; July; Leprosy; Monroe

KEMP, Emily; 34; F; White; Key West; Bahamas; Bahamas; - ;
July; Malarial Fever; Monroe

Name; Age; Sex; Race; Born; FABorn; MOBorn;
        Occup; DODeath; Cause Of Death; County

COLLINS, Alfred W.; 22; M; White; Key West; Ireland; Ireland; -
    ; July; Soft. Of Brain; Monroe
BROWN, Emilio; 1; M; Black; Key West; Bahamas; Bahamas; - ;
    Oct; Marasmus; Monroe
KELLEY, Mary; 8; F; Black; Key West; Key West; Key West; - ;
    Oct; Hypertrophed [unr]; Monroe
ALBRUEY, Irene; 1; F; White; Key West; Bahamas; Bahamas; - ;
    Oct; Convulsions; Monroe
JOHNSON, Infant of Samuel; 1; - ; Black; Key West; Bahamas;
    Bahamas; - ; Oct; Stillborn; Monroe
BRITA, Child of; 1; - ; White; Key West; Cuba; Cuba; - ; Oct;
    Stillborn; Monroe
SWINDELL, John D.; 48; M; White; - ; - ; - ; Laborer; Oct;
    Apoplexy; Monroe
SOMILLAN, Berham B.; 1; M; White; Key West; Cuba; Cuba; - ;
    Oct; Enteritis; Monroe
HIGGS, Infant of Sophia; 1; M; Black; Key West; Bahamas;
    Bahamas; - ; Nov; Stillborn; Monroe
WEATHERFORD, Rosa M.; 1; F; White; Key West; Key West;
    Key West; - ; Nov; Convulsions; Monroe
HICKS, Henrietta; 21; F; White; Key West; Key West; Key West;
    - ; Nov; Consumption; Monroe
ALVAREZ, Henry Wm.; 1; M; Black; Key West; Cuba; Cuba; - ;
    Nov; Gastroenteritis; Monroe
ALBUSEY, child of Elias; 1; M; Black; Key West; Bahamas;
    Bahamas; - ; Nov; Congestive lungs; Monroe
SANTANA, Claudia; 1; M; Black; Key West; Cuba; Cuba; - ;
    Nov; Premature birth; Monroe
VALDEZ, Simian; 1; M; Black; Key West; Cuba; Cuba; - ; Nov;
    Cholera Infection; Monroe
BEYARD, James; 1; M; Black; Key West; Cuba; Cuba; - ; Nov;
    Cholera Infection; Monroe
MURRAY, Mary; 32; F; Black; Nassau; Bahamas; Bahamas;
    Washer; Jan; Convulsions; Monroe
ROBERTS, Webster; 1; M; White; Key West; Key West; Key
    West; - ; Jan; [unreadable]; Monroe
HAVEN, York; 42; M; Black; VA; VA; VA; - ; Jan; Tetanus;
    Monroe

McKEESON, Catherine; 37; F; White; PA; Germany; Germany; -
; Jan; Consumption; Monroe
LOID, Juana; 27; F; White; Key West; Cuba; Cuba; - ; Jan;
Marasmus; Monroe
KENT, Elizabeth; 68; F; White; Bahamas; Bahamas; Bahamas; - ;
Jan; Whooping cough; Monroe
CURRY, Gideon; 34; M; White; Key West; Bahamas; Bahamas; -
; Jan; Chronic Diarrhea; Monroe
ESQUIVEL, Benj.; 23; M; White; Cuba; Cuba; Cuba; - ; Jan;
allum[unreadable]; Monroe
JONES, Robert; 44; M; White; Wales; Wales; Wales; Laborer;
Jan; Bright's Disease; Monroe
PAGET, Louisa; 1; F; White; Key West; Cuba; Cuba; - ; Jan;
Intestinal TB; Monroe
CURRY, Maimie; 15; F; White; Key West; Key West; Key West;
- ; Jan; Heart Disease; Monroe
GONZALEZ, Raimando; 23; M; White; Cuba; Cuba; Cuba;
Cigarmaker; Jan; Consumption; Monroe
MILLIAN,; 1; M; White; Key West; Cuba; Cuba; - ; Feb; Colitis;
Monroe
KEMP, Isadora; 25; F; White; Bahamas; Bahamas; Bahamas; - ;
Feb; Pneumonia; Monroe
LAGUARDIA, Poloride; 67; F; White; Cuba; Cuba; Cuba;
Tobbaco St.; Feb; Pthisis Pulmonary; Monroe
FORD, Lavenia; 1; F; Black; Key West; - ; - ; - ; Feb;
Convulsions; Monroe
CANFIELD, John James; 1; M; White; Key West; - ; - ; - ; Feb;
Pneumonia; Monroe
ARNAO, Josepha; 26; F; White; Cuba; Cuba; Cuba; Tobacco St.;
Feb; Pericarditis; Monroe
HUGHEY, Susan; 52; F; White; GA; GA; GA; - ; May; - ; Orange
GILLIAN, Laura; 21; F; White; TN; TN; TN; - ; Jan; - ; Orange
MCQUAIG, Baby; - ; M; White; FL; AL; GA; - ; June; - ; Orange
BERRY, Nellie; 20; F; White; GA; GA; SC; - ; - ; - ; Orange
POTTS, Missouri; 21; F; White; FL; GA; FL; - ; - ; - ; Orange
RINAULDO, Patti; 44; F; White; VA; VA; VA; - ; Oct;
Consumption; Orange

Name; Age; Sex; Race; Born; FABorn; MOBorn;
            Occup; DODeath; Cause Of Death; County

FLEMING, Capt.; 42; M; White; TN; - ; - ; Real Estate; May;
    Heart Disease; Orange
MOSLEY, Charles; - ; M; White; FL; NY; TN; - ; Nov; Typhoid
    Fever; Orange
TYNER, W. K.; 45; M; White; FL; - ; - ; - ; Feb; Pneumonia;
    Orange
WOODROUGH, Grace L.; 6; F; White; MA; MA; MA; - ; - ;
    Diptheria; Orange
PATRICK, Archibald; 35; M; White; AL; - ; - ; - ; - ;
    Rheumatism; Orange
VEACH, John W.; 63; M; White; - ; - ; - ; - ; - ; Spinal Fever;
    Orange
LEE, T.V.; 39; F; White; - ; - ; - ; - ; - ; Inflamation Bowel; Orange
MCCLAIN, Mary; 45; F; White; FL; - ; - ; - ; - ; Heart Disease;
    Orange
COOPER, Julia; 16; F; Black; - ; - ; - ; - ; - ; Fever; Orange
EDWARDS, Wm.; 10; M; Black; FL; - ; - ; - ; - ; Lightning;
    Orange
BIAS, Samuel; 1; M; White; FL; - ; - ; - ; - ; Inflammation; Orange
GORDON, Betsey; 21; F; Black; FL; - ; - ; - ; - ; Fever; Orange
ANDREWS, Hy; 24; M; Black; MA; - ; - ; - ; - ; Shot Gun;
    Orange
SCHMITZ, Paul; 35; M; White; Indiana; - ; - ; - ; - ; Murdered;
    Orange
CHATTON, Easton; 3; M; Black; MA; - ; - ; - ; - ; Dropsey;
    Orange
SHATTOOK, Geo. F.; 47; M; White; FL; - ; - ; - ; - ; Bronchial
    (?); Orange
JACKMAN, Frank; 20; M; White; FL; - ; - ; - ; - ; Heart Disease;
    Orange
WOOD, Lorine; 56; M; White; FL; - ; - ; - ; - ; Spinal   ; Orange
WASHINGTON, Ellinton; 57; F; Black; GA; - ; - ; - ; - ; General
    Debility; Orange
WHITE, W. G.; 45; M; White; GA; GA; GA; - ; - ; Heart Disease;
    Orange
SCOTT, Maggie; 28; F; White; PA; - ; - ; - ; - ; Typhoid Fever;
    Orange

LEE, Marrion; 23; F; Black; GA; - ; - ; - ; - ; Consumption;
Orange

DeVAUGHN, Eliz.; 30; F; Black; GA; - ; - ; - ; - ; Malarial Fever;
Orange

GILBERT, L (orS). M.; 54; F; White; - ; - ; - ; - ; - ; Consumption;
Orange

BARTON, I. W.; 50; M; White; FL; - ; - ; - ; - ; Heart Disease;
Orange

SEARS, Katie B.; 21; F; White; - ; - ; - ; - ; - ; Fever; Orange

WOODROUGH, Martha; 31; F; White; MA; - ; - ; - ; - ; Malarial
Fever; Orange

JOINER, Neisa; 85; F; White; - ; - ; - ; - ; - ; Old Age; Orange

LEE, Catharine; 103; F; White; - ; - ; - ; - ; - ; Old Age; Orange

BARNHART, L. S.; - ; M; White; FL; GA; FL; - ; June;
Convulsions; Orange

POOLE, R.; 1; M; White; Indiana; IO; CT; - ; Sept; Convulsions;
Orange

McDONALD, Jos.; 83; M; White; Ireland; Ireland; Ireland; - ;
Dec; Gout in legs; Orange

SEYMORE, Marian; 63; F; White; MA; MA; MA; - ; Feb; - ;
Orange

RUIS, Thomas; 38; M; White; - ; - ; - ; - ; Dec; Consumption;
Orange

BRONSON, Henrietta; 12; F; White; FL; GA; GA; - ; Aug; Snake
bite; Orange

GOFF, T.; 46; M; White; - ; - ; - ; - ; Jan; Bright's Disease; Orange

MILE, Robt. H.; 49; M; White; - ; - ; - ; - ; Mar; Consumption;
Orange

CROCE, Kate; 22; F; White; Nova Sco; Nova Sco; Nova Sco; - ;
May; Stoppage of bowel; Orange

HOOPER, L.; 6; F; White; FL; Germany; Germany; - ; Sept; Brain
Fever; Orange

WIMBERLY, Maggie; 15; F; White; FL; SC; Fl; - ; Mar;
Unknown; Orange

TAYLOR, Lawrence; 1; M; Black; FL; FL; FL; - ; July;
Dysentery; Orange

LATTERMORE, Cha.; 12; M; White; FL; FL; FL; - ; Jan;
Malarial Fever; Orange

MITCHELL, B. N.; 68; M; White; GA; - ; - ; Dentist; Mar; Heart
    Disease; Orange

DAVIS, H. M.; 21; F; White; NC; - ; - ; - ; Oct; Convulsions;
    Orange

RING, Lemon; 1; M; Black; GA; SC; GA; - ; Oct; Fever; Orange

ANDERSON, David; 78; M; White; MA; MA; MA; Laborer;
    June; Typhoid Fever; Orange

STEWART. RASTUS; 1; M; White; FL; FL; GA; - ; - ;
    Congestion Brain; Orange

DONNELLY, Sarah; - ; F; White; - ; - ; - ; Washer; Dec; Burnt in
    house; Orange

JANNY, Eva; 32; F; White; MA; MA; MA; - ; Feb; Heart
    Disease; Orange

DEEK, Wm S.; 72; M; White; GA; GA; GA; Farmer; Feb;
    Dropsy/Abcess; Orange

SIMPSON, Eliza; 54; F; White; GA; NC; NC; - ; July; Epilepsy;
    Orange

CONNOR, Jas. W.; 44; M; White; KY; KY; KY; Carpenter; Jan;
    Brain Disease; Orange

SCOTT, Jas. H. ; 57; M; White; IN; DE; KY; Painter; July;
    Dropsey; Orange

DOUGLAS, Jane; 25; F; White; FL; GA; GA; - ; June;
    Cong./Child Bed; Orange

HOLTZCLAW, Jas.; 7; M; White; FL; GA; FL; - ; Feb; Disease of
    bowel; Orange

BRITT, J. C.; 50; M; White; Ireland; - ; - ; Laborer; Sept; Killed;
    Orange

RONEY, Joe C.; 63; M; White; SC; SC; SC; Farmer; July; - ;
    Orange

WILKINS, Cora; 1; F; White; FL; FL; FL; - ; April; - ; Orange

WINKAMAN, Johanna; 49; F; White; Germany; Germany;
    Germany; - ; June; Bronchitis; Orange

LEONOUS, Sallie; 11; F; White; FL; TN; GA; - ; Nov; Gastritis;
    Orange

GRANGE, Pink; 7; M; White; FL; GA; NY; - ; Jan; Acute
    indigestion; Orange

BLANTON, A. T.; 18; F; White; GA; GA; NY; - ; June; Child
    birth comp.; Orange

TIDWELL, Fannie; 17; F; White; FL; - ; - ; - ; Nov; Child bed;
Orange

JORDAN, Wm.; 2; M; Black; FL; GA; GA; - ; Oct; Paralysis;
Orange

SIMMONS, Bessie; 11; F; White; MS; SC; GA; - ; June; Typhoid
Fever; Orange

HILL, Geo. W.; 28; M; White; SC; SC; SC; - ; June; Typhoid
Fever; Orange

HILL, W. (?); 10; M; White; FL; - ; - ; - ; July; Typhoid Fever;
Orange

NEVINS, W. R.; 1; M; White; FL; NY; RI; - ; Dec; Malarial
Fever; Orange

STEPHENS, Anna ; 55; F; White; NY; - ; - ; - ; April; Fever;
Orange

STEVENS, A.; 3; M; White; FL; - ; - ; - ; April; Dysentery;
Orange

HAWKINS, R. D.; 1; M; Black; FL; - ; - ; - ; July; Teething;
Orange

JOINER, M.; 40; M; White; SC; - ; - ; - ; April; Shot Gun; Orange

WILLIE, Prof; 58; M; White; - ; - ; - ; - ; Aug; Fever; Orange

EVANS, Amanda; 27; F; White; GA; - ; - ; - ; June; - ; Orange

STRONG, Bertha; 24; F; Black; - ; - ; - ; - ; Nov; - ; Orange

ROSTER, Tony; 30; M; Black; - ; - ; - ; - ; Nov; - ; Orange

RUTHERFORD, Mat.; 42; F; White; AL; GA; GA; Housekeep;
June; Dysentery; Orange

HOPKINS, C. L.; 29; F; White; OH; OH; OH; - ; May; Chills;
Orange

WHITCOMB, R.; 75; M; White; NY; NY; NY; - ; June; Asthma;
Orange

THORNTON, D. S.; 36; M; White; GA; GA; GA; Machinist; Jan;
Diarrhea; Orange

McCLANNAHAN, Geo.; 24; M; White; OH; OH; OH; RR Agent;
Feb; Hemorrhagic Lung; Orange

THOMPSON, M. L.; 7; F; White; FL; GA; GA; - ; Jan; Diarrhea;
Orange

McCLELLAND, E. M.; 18; F; White; SC; SC; SC; - ; Sept;
Diarrhea; Orange

DYKES, G. P.; 73; M; White; GA; GA; GA; - ; Dec; Heart
    Disease; Orange

BERRY, M B.; 36; F; White; KY; KY; KY; ; Aug; (unreadable);
    Orange

BRACY, M. E.; 18; F; White; SC; SC; SC; - ; Jan; Drowned;
    Orange

HARRIS, A.; 23; F; White; Canada; Canada; Canada; - ; June;
    Fever; Orange

WILDEMAN, E. R.; 40; M; White; NY; NY; NY; Orange gr.;
    May; Falling tree; Orange

SWISHER, Jas.; 45; M; White; PA; PA; PA; - ; Feb;
    Consumption; Orange

RANIE, Willie L.; 6; M; White; FL; MA; SC; - ; Sept; Inflam of
    bowels; Orange

WOOD, B.; 24; F; White; MA; MA; MA; - ; Feb; Blood poison;
    Orange

WILEY, G.; 13; F; White; FL; GA; GA; - ; May; Measles; Orange

DRUGGORS, E.; 40; F; White; FL; GA; GA; - ; April;
    Consumption; Orange

RAYBORN, M. L.; 1; F; White; FL; GA; GA; - ; Aug; Miningitis;
    Orange

ANDERSON, M. F.; 2; F; White; GA; GA; GA; - ; Oct;
    Dysentery; Polk

SURRENCY, Infant; - ; M; White; FL; GA; GA; - ; May;
    Unknown; Polk

CARRUTHERS, D. H.; 1; M; White; FL; GA; GA; - ; Jan;
    Dysentery; Polk

MILLS, G. M.; 4; F; White; FL; FL; FL; - ; June; Erysipelas; Polk

LANNIE, Lewis; 74; M; White; GA; GA; GA; Farmer; Dec;
    Congestive Chills; Polk

TILLIS, Rubie; 1; F; M; FL; FL; FL; - ; April; Dysentery; Polk

MINOR, L. A.; 39; F; White; VA; MD; MD; - ; April; Dysentery;
    Polk

BLOOM, L. A.; 12; F; White; FL; NC; FL; - ; April; Poisoned;
    Polk

PEOPLES, M. A.; 59; F; White; GA; GA; SC; Doctors; Oct; Heart
    Disease; Polk

EVERETT, Henry; 40; M; White; NC; NC; NC; Professor; June;
Congestion; Polk

PETERS, W. S.; 69; M; White; SC; SC; SC; Blacksmith; Aug;
Heart Disease; Polk

HART, Bruce; 1; M; White; FL; GA; GA; - ; Mar; Flux; Polk

JOHNSON, Laura F.; 12; F; White; FL; GA; GA; - ; Oct;
Congestion Brain; Polk

BOSWORTH, Frances L.; 1; F; White; FL; NY; FL; - ; July;
Falling; Polk

WILCHER, Wm. T.; 1; M; White; FL; VA; TN; - ; May;
Pneumonia; Polk

HULL, Belle; 1; F; White; FL; FL; GA; - ; Dec; Malarial Fever;
Polk

NEWMAN, Louisa; 30; F; White; GA; GA; GA; Washerwom;
Mar; Gun shot wound; Polk

TRASK, Georgia E.; 6; F; White; FL; FL; FL; - ; Feb; Pneumonia;
Polk

COX, C.; 12; M; White; GA; GA; GA; Farmer; Mar; Dysentery;
Polk

COX, L.; 9; F; White; GA; GA; GA; - ; Mar; Dysentery; Polk

COX, B. A.; 6; F; White; FL; GA; GA; - ; Mar; Dysentery; Polk

COX, Dallie; 1; F; White; FL; GA; GA; - ; Mar; Dysentery; Polk

FERNALD, L. M.; 26; F; White; NJ; NJ; NJ; Housekeep; May;
Child Birth; Polk

SNELLINGER, O. M.; 1; M; White; FL; MD; PN; - ; May; - ;
Polk

TURNER, W. H.; 5; M; White; FL; FL; FL; - ; Dec; Dysentery;
Polk

TURNER, N.; 1; M; White; FL; FL; FL; - ; Dec; Dysentery; Polk

CAMPBELL, O. J.; 15; M; White; FL; FL; FL; Farmer; Dec;
Dysentery; Polk

LUNN, (no first name given); 1; M; White; FL; GA; GA; - ; Dec;
Dysentery; Polk

MOORE, W. D.; 1; M; White; FL; VA; FL; - ; Nov; Dysentery;
Polk

CASTRINE, Mandy; 27; F; White; FL; - ; - ; - ; Feb; - ; Polk

RILEY, James; 36; M; White; Ireland; Ireland; Ireland; Peddler;
May; Consumption; Polk

BOND, Rosina; 45; F; White; MS; SC; - ; Housewife; April;
     Consumption; Polk
DUCKWORTH, Van; 1; M; White; FL; IN; MD; - ; Dec;
     Dysentery; Polk
ROBINS, A. B.; 1; F; White; AL; AL; AL; - ; Aug; Teething; Polk
GILBERT, Lewis; 40; M; White; TN; VT; NC; M. D.; May; Lung
     Fever; Polk
SMITH, Rosa; 2; F; White; FL; GA; GA; - ; Oct; Dysentery; Polk
JOHNSON, Mary; 3; F; Black; FL; FL; FL; - ; Mar; Brain Fever;
     Putnam
McLEOD, Juda; 26; F; Black; GA; GA; SC; - ; Nov; Pneumonia;
     Putnam
TUCKER, A. A.; 30; - ; White; SC; SC; SC; - ; - ; Apoplexy;
     Putnam
TUCKER, W. L. ; 40; M; White; SC; SC; SC; Fruit Grow; Mar;
     Rheumatism; Putnam
TUCKER, J. W. L.; 66; M; White; SC; SC; SC; Fruit Grow; Apr;
     Heart Disease; Putnam
COLLINS, Rev.; 45; M; White; England; England; England;
     Minister; May; Lung Disease; Putnam
CANNADY, James; 30; M ; White; SC; SC; SC; Barber; Dec;
     Typhoid Fever; Putnam
MILLER, Mrs. J.; 25; F; White; MA; MA; MA; - ; Aut; Child bed
     fever; Putnam
SPRAGUE, Katie; 42; F; White; SC; SC; SC; - ; Nov; Dysentery;
     Putnam
KENYAN, Martin; 26; M; White; MA; MA; MA; Capt. Boat;
     May; Lung Disease; Putnam
GASTON, Sallie; 4; F; Black; FL; FL; FL; - ; Dec; Dysentery;
     Putnam
CHASE, Lillie; 14; F; White; ME; ME; ME; Student; May; Acc.
     Burned; Putnam
HARSHMAN, Mary; 22; F; White; NY; ENG; NY; - ; July; Child
     birth; Putnam
GALE, James; 12; M; White; NY; NY; NY; - ; Dec; Dropsey;
     Putnam
GALE, Miss Olie; 2; F; White; FL; England; NY; - ; Aug;
     Dysentery; Putnam

STEPHENS, Burt; 70; M; Black; GA; GA; GA; Laborer; Dec; Heart Disease; Putnam

AINSLEY, Robert; 45; M; White; TN; TN; TN; Dentist; Dec; Hepatitis; Putnam

STEPHENS, Carrie; 22; F; White; NY; NY; NY; - ; May; Convulsions; Putnam

OLMSTEAD, Mrs. Ed; 40; F; White; NY; NY; NY; - ; Dec; Child Birth; Putnam

WILLIAMS, Ellen; 22; F; White; MA; MA; MA; - ; Dec; Lung Disease; Putnam

MAULL, Charlie; 13; M; White; GA; GA; GA; - ; May; Lightening; Putnam

LONG, Solan; 8; M; White; FL; SC; SC; - ; Jan; Dysentery; Putnam

LANAIRS, Lizzie; 20; F; White; FL; FL; FL; - ; Dec; Child Birth; Putnam

COMES (?), Clifton; 18; M; White; MA; MA; MA; Fruit Grow; Apr; Suicide (shot); Putnam

LOVELACE, Susan; 40; F; White; Canada; Canada; Canada; - ; Apr; Meningitis; Putnam

FLOYD, Blanch; 2; F; Black; FL; NC; GA; - ; Oct; Fever; Putnam

LEE, Gracy; 5; F; Black; FL; FL; FL; - ; Dec; Acc. Poison; Putnam

JACKSON, Thos.; 1; M; Black; FL; FL; FL; - ; Feb; Fever; Putnam

WAGNER, Alex; 65; M; Black; NC; NC; NC; Laborer; May; Typhoid Fever; Putnam

SPENCER, Hannah; 20; F; Black; FL; FL; FL; Laborer; Oct; Fever; Putnam

BAILE, D.; 48; M; White; MA; MA; MA; M.D.; July; Lung Disease; Putnam

HODGES, Mrs. H.; 23; F; White; MA; MA; MA; - ; Aug; Child Birth; Putnam

CLARK, Charles; 34; M; White; CT; Foreign; Foreign; Cotton; Nov; Brain Disease; Putnam

HART, Walter N.; 42; M; White; NY; NY; NY; Farmer; July; Heart Disease; Putnam

Name; Age; Sex; Race; Born; FABorn; MOBorn;
        Occup; DODeath; Cause Of Death; County

EVANS, William J.; 8; M; White; FL; VA; NY; - ; July; Cholera
Infection; Putnam
McLEOD, Dan; 51; M; White; GA; GA; GA; Farmer; Nov;
Pneumonia; Putnam
JENKINS, Willie; 7; M; Black; FL; FL; SC; - ; May; Typhoid
Fever; Putnam
PORTER, Mr.; 33; M; White; GA; GA; GA; - ; May; Pulm.
Cong.; Putnam
BRANCH, Ira; 1; M; Black; FL; GA; FL; - ; May; Colitis; Putnam
DUNHAM, Cassie; 1; F; White; FL; NY; FL; - ; June; Cong.
Bowels; Putnam
CLARK, James K.; 50; M; White; CT; CT; CT; - ; June;
Consumption; Putnam
BRICKELL, Elsworth; 22; M; White; IL; IL; IL; - ; June; Typhoid
Fever; Putnam
JENSKO, Ladny Patsy; 1; M; White; FL; Germany; Germany; - ;
July; Cholera Infection; Putnam
HUNTER, Fannie; 3; F; Black; SC; SC; SC; - ; July; Fever;
Putnam
McLANRY, Susan; 13; F; White; WI; WI; WI; - ; July; Typhoid
Fever; Putnam
MONTELL, Ponssee; 55; F; White; SC; SC; SC; - ; July; Fever;
Putnam
WILSON, Sarah A.; 60; F; White; CT; CT; CT; - ; July; Fever;
Putnam
CALVIN, L.; 30; M; Black; GA; GA; GA; - ; July; Malarial
Fever; Putnam
RADCLIFFE, A. R.; 28; M; White; - ; - ; - ; - ; July; Delirium ;
Putnam
BLACK, Jessie; 15; M; Black; FL; - ; - ; - ; Aug; Phthisis; Putnam
MILLER, Emily; 28; F; White; SC; SC; SC; - ; Aug; Fever;
Putnam
JACKSON, John; 40; M; Black; - ; - ; - ; - ; Aug; Pistol Shot;
Putnam
HUNTER, Alexander; 13; M; Black; SC; SC; SC; - ; Aug;
Pneumonia; Putnam
AMBOURG, John; 28; M; White; NY; NY; NY; - ; Sept; Typhoid
Fever; Putnam

MORSE, A. D.; 52; M; White; MA; - ; - ; - ; Sept; - ; Putnam

ROSS, Maggie; 20; F; Black; SC; SC; SC; - ; Oct; Phthisis; Putnam

GREEN, Mary A.; 27; F; White; FL; FL; FL; - ; Oct; Unknown; Putnam

PETERMAN, Annie M.; 23; F; White; FL; ENG; ENG; - ; Oct; Malarial Fever; Putnam

BUCKLE, John W.; 28; M; Black; GA; GA; GA; - ; Oct; Malarial Fever; Putnam

WASHINGTON, Mary J.; 36; F; Black; FL; GA; AL; - ; Aug; Lung Disease; Putnam

CRONAN, Thomas; 27; M; White; IL; IL; IL; Laborer; Aug; Shot; Putnam

RUMLEY, Mattie; 16; F; White; IL; NC; NC; - ; July; Typhoid Fever; Putnam

RUMLEY, George; 14; M; White; IL; NC; NC; - ; Aug; Typhoid Fever; Putnam

SKINNER, Robert W.; 27; M; White; GA; GA; GA; Laborer; Aug; Inflam. Bowels; Putnam

MITCHELL, John; 1; M; Black; FL; FL; FL; Laborer; April; Spasms; Putnam

WHIPP, Susan A.; 32; F; White; PA; PA; PA; - ; May; Child Birth; Putnam

GREEN, N. B.; 35; M; White; FL; FL; FL; Fruit Grow; Sept; Typhoid Fever; Putnam

RICKS, Martha; 30; F; White; GA; GA; GA; - ; July; Malarial Fever; Putnam

PARKHILL, Sisie; 1; F; White; FL; FL; FL; - ; Nov; Malarial Fever; Putnam

KING, Lanina; 30; F; White; FL; FL; FL; - ; Nov; Bright's Disease; Putnam

GREEN, Herman; 1; M; White; FL; FL; FL; - ; June; Typhoid Fever; Putnam

MAZELL, Johnie; 1; M; White; FL; FL; FL; - ; May; Heart; Putnam

CARROLL, Press; 27; M; Black; SC; SC; SC; Laborer; Mar; Shot in fracas; Putnam

Name; Age; Sex; Race; Born; FABorn; MOBorn;
        Occup; DODeath; Cause Of Death; County

RYNE, Mrs.; 30; F; White; NY; NY; NY; - ; April; Lung Disease;
    Putnam
BAXLEY, Sisie; 1; F; White; FL; SC; SC; - ; July; Diptheria;
    Putnam
WATSON, Loduskey; 18; F; White; FL; Al; AL; - ; Nov; Typhoid
    Fever; Putnam
PEARSON, Brooks; 25; M; White; SC; SC; SC; - ; Mar;
    Congestion; Putnam
WILLIAMS, Cornelius; 18; F; Black; FL; FL; FL; - ; Mar; Child
    Birth; Putnam
JOHNSON, Rev. William; 82; M; White; SC; SC; SC; Minister;
    Dec; Chron. Diarrhea; Putnam
LOVELACE, Martha; 45; F; White; SC; SC; SC; - ; Sept;
    Dropsey; Putnam
LEGGINS, Robert; 14; M; Black; FL; FL; SC; - ; Aug;
    Consumption; Putnam
LEGGINS, William; 12; M; Black; FL; FL; SC; - ; July;
    Consumption; Putnam
HOLMES, Mary; 21; F; Black; FL; FL; FL; - ; July ; Lung
    Disease; Putnam
MARM, John; 4; M; White; FL; GA; GA; - ; Mar; Laryngitis;
    Putnam
PORTER, Virginia; 28; F; White; FL; GA; GA; - ; June; Typhoid
    Fever; Putnam
CADE, W. W.; 24; M; White; FL; SC; SC; Farmer; Sept; Typhoid
    Fever; Putnam
CADE, C. M.; 22; M; White; FL; SC; SC; Farmer; Oct; Typhoid
    Fever; Putnam
COTTIN, Preston; 1; M; White; FL; GA; GA; - ; June; Dysentery;
    Putnam
McRAE, W. E.; 2; M; White; FL; SC; SC; - ; April; Brain
    Congestion; Putnam
WESTGARDE, Emma; 7; F; White; PA; Norway; England; - ;
    Jan; Malarial Fever; Putnam
SPARKMAN, Lydia; 86; F; White; SC; SC; SC; - ; April;
    Paralysis; Putnam
STRICKLAND, Judson; 28; M; White; FL; SC; SC; Sch. Super; -
    ; Lung Disease; Putnam

VARNES, Julia; 36; F; White; FL; FL; FL; - ; Dec; Typhoid
Fever; Putnam

BOHANNON, Cornelia; 18; F; White; FL; GA; GA; - ; June;
Pneumonia; Putnam

BUNDY, Clarence; 6; M; White; FL; FL; FL; - ; Dec; Typhoid
Fever; Putnam

BUNDY, Idella; 4; F; White; FL; FL; FL; - ; Oct; Typhoid Fever;
Putnam

JOHNS, Luke; 72; M; White; GA; GA; GA; Farmer; Apr; Brain
Congestion; Putnam

HOLT, David; 60; M; White; AL; VA; AL; Farmer; May; Heart
Disease; Santa Rosa

CANNON, Henry; 65; M; White; AL; AL; SC; Teacher; Nov;
Heart Disease; Santa Rosa

PEADEN, Catherine; 30; F; White; FL; FL; FL; - ; Feb;
Pneumonia; Santa Rosa

CARR, Davy; 3; M; White; FL; FL; FL; - ; Mar; Unknown; Santa
Rosa

GARRETT, Mineola; 8; F; White; FL; AL; AL; - ; July; Worms;
Santa Rosa

FRANKLIN, Virginia; 17; F; White; FL; FL; FL; - ; May; Child
Birth; Santa Rosa

FRANKLIN, Baby; 1; F; White; FL; FL; FL; - ; May; - ; Santa
Rosa

FORBES, S. S. ; 58; M; White; NY; NY; NY; Physician; Aug;
Heart Disease; Santa Rosa

LILINS, H. J.; 2; M; White; FL; AL; AL; - ; June; Marasmus;
Santa Rosa

McLELLAN, Babe; 1; M; White; FL; Scotland; Scotland; - ; Oct;
(?) dentition; Santa Rosa

BOGBRICK, F; 89; M; White; Austria; Austria; Austria; Seaman;
Nov; Cancer/stomach; Santa Rosa

MARTIN, W. D.; 66; M; White; - ; - ; - ; Jailer; Nov; Heart
Disease; Santa Rosa

ALBURY, Chas.; 80; M; White; FL; FL; FL; Railroad; Dec;
Fever; Santa Rosa

COLLINS, Mrs. M.; 92; F; White; FL; SC; SC; - ; Aug; Old Age;
Santa Rosa

Name; Age; Sex; Race; Born; FABorn; MOBorn;
          Occup; DODeath; Cause Of Death; County

FLEMING, Mrs. J.; 95; F; White; GA; GA; GA; - ; Oct; Old Age;
     Santa Rosa
INMES, Mrs. L.; 77; F; White; TN; - ; - ; - ; Oct; Old Age; Santa
     Rosa
NELSON, Jno.; 11; M; White; FL; FL; FL; - ; May; drowned;
     Santa Rosa
MARBRY, Wm.; 45; M; White; FL; FL; AL; Cook; May;
     Pernicious Fever; Santa Rosa
MONROE, H. C.; 26; M; Black; FL; FL; FL; - ; Jan; Pernicious
     Fever; Santa Rosa
STEELE, Robt.; 69; M; White; AL; SC; SC; Farmer; Mar;
     Sudden; Santa Rosa
KING, T. J.; 38; M; White; AL; Al; AL; Laborer; Jan; Killed by
     accident; Santa Rosa
JACKSON, Louis; 70; M; Black; - ; - ; - ; Bricklayer; Oct; Bilious
     Fever; Santa Rosa
FAULK, A.; 75; M; White; - ; SC; GA; Farmer; Nov; Old Age;
     Santa Rosa
BRAY, Benj.; 75; M; White; SC; SC; SC; Farmer; Mar; Dropsy of
     chest; Santa Rosa
ABRO, Virginia F.; 77; F; White; FL; AL; FL; - ; Mar; Pernicious
     Fever; Santa Rosa
FAULK, A.; 35; M; White; FL; GA; SC; Farmer; Aug;
     Intussusception; Santa Rosa
HALL, Ida; 24; F; White; FL; AL; AL; - ; Feb; Pernicious Fever;
     Santa Rosa
EDGARS, Jms.; 45; M; White; AL; AL; AL; Farmer; Feb;
     Murdered; Santa Rosa
JERNIGAN, Jesse; 2; M; White; FL; FL; FL; - ; Feb; Teething;
     Santa Rosa
LAWLER, Alexander; 16; M; White; FL; Ireland; FL; - ; Mar;
     Fever; St. Johns
HARTGROVE, Martha; 76; F; White; SC; SC; SC; - ; Apr;
     Consumption; St. Johns
PALMER, Fanny; 1; F; White; FL; NY; NY; - ; Apr; - ; St. Johns
ADAMS, Deed; 22; M; Black; FL; FL; FL; - ; Apr; Drowned; St.
     Johns

CASSON, Clorida; 60; F; White; FL; FL; FL; - ; Apr; Paralysis; St. Johns

NATILE, Frank; 25; M; Black; FL; FL; FL; Laborer; May; Consumption; St. Johns

JOYCE, Fanny; 1; F; White; NY; NY; NY; - ; - ; Fever; St. Johns

CROSLEY, Jeremiah; 1; M; Black; FL; FL; FL; - ; June; Cold; St. Johns

MASON, R.; 1; M; Black; FL; FL; FL; - ; June; Unknown; St. Johns

LOPEZ, Hattie; 1; F; White; FL; FL; FL; - ; June; Fever; St. Johns

THYNE, Isabel; 54; F; White; FL; FL; FL; - ; July; Fever; St. Johns

FORTANY, B.; 30; M; Black; FL; FL; FL; - ; July; Fever; St. Johns

LOPEZ, Eloyse; 2; F; White; FL; FL; FL; - ; July; Worms; St. Johns

BAILEY, Frank; 1; M; Black; FL; FL; FL; - ; July; Cold; St. Johns

MICKLER, Jackson; 22; M; White; FL; FL; FL; - ; July; Lock Jaw; St. Johns

McKINNEY, J. T.; 1; M; Black; FL; FL; FL; - ; July; Diarrhea; St. Johns

ADAMS, James; 1; F; Black; FL; FL; FL; - ; Aug; Cold; St. Johns

STINER, Edward; 1; M; Black; FL; FL; FL; - ; Sept; Cold; St. Johns

BUNTING, Maud; 2; F; White; FL; VA; NC; - ; Sept; Cold; St. Johns

NATILE, Phillis; 90; F; Black; FL; FL; FL; - ; Sept; Old Age; St. Johns

WARREN, Lina; 1; F; Black; FL; FL; FL; - ; Oct; Cold; St. Johns

WING, P.; 1; M; Black; FL; FL; FL; - ; Oct; Fever; St. Johns

TARBOX, R. W.; 52; M; White; GA; GA; GA; - ; Oct; Consumption; St. Johns

HALSEY, James; 53; M; White; NY; NY; NY; - ; Oct; Consumption; St. Johns

LOPEZ, Mrs. D.; 33; F; White; FL; FL; FL; - ; Oct; Consumption; St. Johns

SESION, Serby; 1; M; Black; FL; FL; FL; - ; Nov; Cold; St. Johns

Name; Age; Sex; Race; Born; FABorn; MOBorn;
        Occup; DODeath; Cause Of Death; County

WARREN, Caroline; 70; F; Black; FL; FL; FL; - ; Nov;
    Unknown; St. Johns
WILLIAMS, Samm; 26; M; White; FL; FL; FL; - ; Nov;
    Consumption; St. Johns
OWENS, James; 1; M; White; FL; GA; FL; - ; Nov; Cold; St.
    Johns
RANDLE, Rustus; 71; M; White; - ; - ; - ; - ; Nov; Asthma; St.
    Johns
EDGAR, Dan'l; 67; M; White; NY; NY; NY; - ; Nov; None listed;
    St. Johns
RUSSELL, Edward; 67; M; White; FL; FL; FL; - ; Dec;
    Consumption; St. Johns
NEUMAN, John; 8; M; Black; FL; FL; FL; - ; Dec; Lock Jaw; St.
    Johns
UPDYKE, Manuel; 1; M; White; FL; FL; FL; - ; Jan; None listed;
    St. Johns
MARTIN, Casemire; 53; M; White; FL; FL; FL; - ; Jan; Cancer;
    St. Johns
WELLS, Hubert; 1; M; Black; FL; FL; FL; - ; Feb; Worms; St.
    Johns
SCOTT, W. B.; 72; M; Black; FL; FL; FL; - ; Feb; Consumption;
    St. Johns
MARTEN, Mercy; 85; F; Black; FL; FL; FL; - ; Feb; Old Age; St.
    Johns
GOMEZ, H. S.; 30; M; Black; FL; FL; FL; - ; Feb; Consumption;
    St. Johns
EASTON, Chas. P.; 60; M; Black; FL; FL; FL; - ; Mar; Astha; St.
    Johns
EDWARD, Mrs. I. T.; 44; F; White; FL; FL; FL; - ; Mar;
    Vertebrae; St. Johns
TUCKER, Chas. P.; 51; M; Black; FL; FL; FL; - ; Mar;
    Consumption; St. Johns
LAWLER, Mrs. Michael; 60; F; White; FL; FL; FL; - ; Mar;
    Fever; St. Johns
WILLIAMSON, (none given); 1; F; White; FL; GA; GA; - ; Dec;
    Stillborn; Sumter
LEWIS, Lula; 1; F; Black; FL; GA; SC; - ; June; Croup; Sumter

ABBAGE, John; 60; W; Mu; unknown; unknown; unknown;
Farmer; Dec; Paralysis; Sumter

OLANDY, Hope; 35; W; F; GA; - ; - ; - ; May; Child Birth;
Sumter

CARTER, Alice May; 3; F; White; FL; FL; FL; - ; Aug;
Congestion/bowel; Sumter

FURRMAN, C. J.; 2; F; White; SC; SC; Germany; - ; Jan;
Convulsions; Sumter

COLLINS, Delilah; 39; F; White; FL; GA; GA; - ; Aug;
Hemorrhagic Fever; Sumter

DAVIES, Wm.; 62; M; White; GA; GA; GA; Minister; Apr;
Paralysis; Sumter

TURNAGE, W. R.; 1; M; White; FL; FL; FL; - ; Mar; Dysentery;
Sumter

WHITMAN, Jacob; 60; M; White; FL; GA; FL; Farmer; Mar;
Dropsey; Sumter

COLLINS, Wright; 70; M; White; GA; - ; - ; Farmer; Jan;
Desepsia; Sumter

BRADFORD, Jos. T.; 3; M; White; FL; FL; GA; - ; May; Typhoid
Fever; Sumter

OLIVER, (none given); 100; F; White; FL; GA; GA; - ; Dec; - ;
Sumter

LIVINGSTON, Cope; 38; M; Black; FL; GA; GA; Framer; - ;
Fractured thigh; Sumter

GOUGH, Amanda; 24; F; Black; FL; FL; FL; - ; Dec; Child Birth;
Sumter

GOUGH, Columbus; 37; M; White; FL; NY; FL; Farmer; July;
Epilepsy; Sumter

GOUGH, James; 9; M; White; FL; FL; FL; - ; July; Dropsey;
Sumter

GOUGH, John; 5; M; White; FL; FL; FL; - ; July; Congestion;
Sumter

HULL, Mertie; 6; F; White; MO; OH; MO; - ; June; - ; Sumter

HULL, (none given); - ; M; White; FL; OH; MO; - ; June;
Stillborn; Sumter

THOMAS, (none given); - ; F; White; FL; - ; - ; - ; June; Epilepsy;
Sumter

Name; Age; Sex; Race; Born; FABorn; MOBorn;
        Occup; DODeath; Cause Of Death; County

CHILDERS, Chas.; 30; M; White; AL; TN; GA; Farmer; Sept;
    Kidney; Sumter
SEALE, E. B.; 32; F; White; MS; VA; MS; - ; Nov; Cong of
    stomach; Sumter
AIKINS, Sarah; 28; F; White; FL; GA; GA; - ; Oct; Child birth;
    Sumter
AIKINS, Mary A.; 3; F; White; FL; GA; FL; - ; Mar; Cancer;
    Sumter
HALL, (none given); 1; M; White; FL; GA; FL; - ; Apr; Hives;
    Sumter
SHECRET, J. E.; 40; F; White; GA; GA; GA; - ; Sept; Overdose
    morphi; Sumter
MALLARD, R. B.; 30; F; White; FL; NC; NC; - ; June; Suicide
    (shot); Sumter
MALLARD, Robt.; 3; M; White; FL; AL; FL; - ; June; Fever;
    Sumter
KIMBROUGH, G. M. C.; 1; M; White; FL; GA; GA; - ; Aug;
    Dysentery; Sumter
KIMBROUGH, A.; 4; M; White; GA; GA; GA; - ; Sept; Shot by
    accident; Sumter
SLOAN, L. L. ; 9; M; White; FL; GA; FL; - ; Oct; Congestive
    fever; Sumter
LOVE, M. M.; 39; F; White; MS; AL; AL; - ; May; Typhoid
    Fever; Sumter
WILLIAMS, Peter; 51; M; Black; SC; - ; - ; Farmer; Feb; - ;
    Sumter
TESTON, Margaret; 54; F; White; GA; GA; GA; - ; Oct; Bright's
    Disease; Sumter
WIGGINS, J. R.; 11; M; White; FL; GA; AL; - ; Nov;
    Hemorrhagic fever; Sumter
RAAKES, Willie; 2; M; White; FL; AL; AL; - ; Nov; Congestion
    brain; Sumter
EASTMAN, H. C.; 72; F; White; CT; MS; CT; Farmer; Sept;
    Paralysis brain; Sumter
ROBBINS, L. C.; 15; M; White; FL; AL; AL; - ; Aug; Dropsey;
    Sumter
SNOW, Ida; 1; F; White; FL; GA; FL; - ; July; Pneumonia;
    Sumter

KNIGHT, D. H.; 6; M; White; FL; FL; FL; - ; May; Dropsey of heart; Sumter

HOPSON, S. A. E.; 31; F; White; GA; FL; GA; - ; Sept; Bilious dysentery; Sumter

GOUGH,T. E.; 7; M; White; FL; GA; GA; - ; Nov; Burnt; Sumter

DOUGLAS, A. A.; 5; M; White; FL; GA; FL; - ; Feb; Cong of brain; Sumter

WILLIAMS, Alice W.; 39; F; White; KY; KY; KY; - ; Mar; Worm's disease; Sumter

COLLEY, J. B.; 66; M; White; AL; TN; TN; - ; Aug; Dysentery; Sumter

WEBB, L. E.; 45; M; White; VA; VA; VA; - ; Apr; Dysentery; Sumter

McGEHEE, Ella; 18; F; White; TN; TN; TN; - ; July; Blood in head; Sumter

COOPER, John; 51; M; White; England; England; England; - ; Aug; Dysentery; Sumter

RICKARD, (none given); 60; M; White; PA; PA; PA; - ; Mar; Diabetes; Sumter

ANDERSON, Gus; 28; M; White; Sweden; Sweden; Sweden; - ; July; Convulsions; Sumter

MATHEWS, Frank; 20; M; Black; NC; NC; NC; - ; Dec; Drowning; Sumter

WILLIS, Henry; 17; M; Black; FL; - ; VA; Laborer; Nov; Cough; Sumter

AIKINS, Infant; 1; F; Black; FL; SC; GA; - ; May; Stillborn; Sumter

BEVILLE, Josephine; 4; F; Mu; FL; - ; FL; - ; Oct; Chills and fever; Sumter

REIVES, Charles; 1; M; Mu; - ; - ; - ; - ; Aug; - ; Sumter

HUMPHREYS, M. P.; 46; F; White; MO; Ireland; KY; - ; June; Inflam. Bowels; Sumter

BECKET, N. J.; 23; M; White; MS; - ; - ; - ; Apr; Measles; Sumter

YOUNG, (none given); - ; - ; - ; FL; GA; GA; - ; May; Hives; Sumter

CURRY; - ; - ; - ; SC; SC; SC; Farmer; Oct; Cong of liver; Sumter

DeHAW, Maud; - ; - ; - ; FL; AL; AL; - ; Sept; Dysentery; Sumter

Name; Age; Sex; Race; Born; FABorn; MOBorn;
          Occup; DODeath; Cause Of Death; County

ARMSTRONG, Barry; - ; - ; - ; MS; TN; MS; - ; Nov;
     Consumption; Sumter
HODGES, N. S.; - ; - ; - ; GA; GA; GA; - ; Sept; Cong fever;
     Sumter
McEASHEM, (none given); 1; F; White; FL; - ; - ; - ; Feb;
     Consumption; Sumter
LARKINS, B. M.; 62; M; White; KY; PA; IL; Physician; May;
     Bowel Complaint; Sumter
SLATER, Roy; 1; M; White; FL; - ; - ; - ; Nov; - ; Sumter
BARRAM, (none given); - ; M; White; MI; AL; Al; Farmer; June;
     Spinal Affection; Sumter
COOK, Wm. D.; 26; M; White; AL; MA; MA; - ; July; Paralysis;
     Sumter
EASTMAN, H. C.; 13; F; White; CT; AL; AL; - ; Aug;
     Congestive fever; Sumter
COLEMAN, Daisy; 12; F; White; AL; MS; MS; - ; June;
     Congestive fever; Sumter
TAYLOR, Louise; 6; F; White; MI; - ; - ; - ; Aug; Congestive
     fever; Sumter
GARRISON, Jas.; 31; M; White; IN; GA; AL; Blacksmith; Oct;
     Congestive fever; Sumter
FUSSELL, Mary; 7; F; White; FL; MS; AL; - ; Jan; Effects
     (unread.); Sumter
PEACOCK, Wesley; 2; M; White; MS; - ; - ; - ; Nov; Dysentery;
     Sumter
HARMON, Ellis; 47; M; White; KY; - ; - ; Farmer; July; Kidney
     Disease; Sumter
GAMBLE, M. A.; 73; F; White; SC; - ; - ; - ; May; Bilirous Fever;
     Sumter
CRAFT, Maria; 40; F; White; AL; OH; OH; - ; May; - ; Sumter
JONES, (none given); 1; M; White; FL; GA; GA; - ; Oct;
     Stillborn; Sumter
GIDEMS, G.; 29; M; White; GA; CT; Nova Sco.; - ; June;
     Congestive fever; Sumter
OSBORN, S. L.; 1; F; White; CT; KY; KY; - ; Apr; Dysentery;
     Sumter
McLENDON, Jm.; 3; M; White; FL; AL; KY; - ; Aug;
     Pulmonary; Sumter

LANIER, Laura M.; 1; F; White; FL; AL; KY; - ; Apr; Congestion
bowel; Sumter

LANIER, Alice E.; 24; F; White; FL; CT; CT; - ; June;
Pneumonia; Sumter

HUBBARD, F. D.; 1; M; White; CT; CT; FL; - ; Mar; Congestive
fever; Sumter

STROUDER, Minnie; 1; F; White; FL; AL; AL; - ; Apr; Teething;
Sumter

GARDEN, Luray Lee; 30; F; White; OH; OH; OH; - ; Feb;
Dysentery; Sumter

KNOWLES, (none given); 21; F; White; FL; GA; GA; - ; July;
Childbirth prob.; Sumter

UNGH, Ruth; 41; F; White; MS; MS; MS; - ; July; Abortion;
Sumter

DUNCAN, Jennie; 35; F; White; KY; KY; KY; - ; Apr; Gastritis;
Sumter

CHILD, J. N.; 48; M; White; VA; VA; VA; - ; Dec; Dysentery;
Sumter

LANIER, (?) C.; 1; F; White; FL; GA; GA; - ; Mar; Cholera
Infection; Sumter

LEE, Sarah; 38; F; White; GA; - ; GA; - ; Feb; Pneumonia; Sumter

MYERS, F.; 31; F; White; SC; - ; - ; - ; Apr; Pneumonia; Sumter

CASEY, Naomi; 23; F; White; KY; - ; - ; - ; Oct; Dysentery;
Sumter

SHANKLIN, J. R.; 21; M; White; GA; AL; GA; Laborer; Jul;
Malarial Fever; Sumter

MILLER, C. V.; 45; F; White; AL; AL; AL; - ; Sept; Rheumatism;
Sumter

MILAM, L. B.; 11; M; White; TN; TN; TN; - ; Apr; Malarial
Fever; Sumter

HODGES, S. B.; 10; F; White; GA; SC; GA; Farmer; Oct;
Malarial Fever; Sumter

HODGES, C. L.; 1; F; White; FL; SC; GA; - ; Sept; Consumption;
Sumter

BATES, L. P.; 2; F; White; AL; AL; TN; - ; Sept; Dysentery;
Sumter

BATES, L. A.; 1; F; White; AL; AL; TN; - ; Sept; Dysentery;
Sumter

Name; Age; Sex; Race; Born; FABorn; MOBorn;
        Occup; DODeath; Cause Of Death; County

THORN, Quilla; 1; F; White; TX; AL; GA; - ; Nov; Dysentery;
    Sumter
LEWIS, Eugena; 1; M; White; FL; SC; FL; - ; Feb; Dropsey;
    Sumter
BLAIR, Montgomery; 16; M; White; FL; GA; AL; - ; Nov;
    Rheumatism; Sumter
PERRY, L. A.; 1; F; White; FL; SC; FL; - ; Apr; Dysentery;
    Sumter
STAPLETON, Young; 1; M; White; FL; AL; AL; - ; Apr; Catarrh;
    Sumter
WALKING, Nellie; 1; F; White; FL; SC; FL; - ; May; Dysentery;
    Sumter
HALL, T. G.; 6; M; White; SC; SC; SC; - ; Jun; Dysentery;
    Sumter
WALKER, M. M.; 1; F; White; FL; GA; FL; - ; Nov; Congestion
    bowel; Sumter
COOPER, Katie; 1; F; White; FL; AL; AL; - ; Mar; Spinal
    Affection; Sumter
GRANT, Frank; 55; M; White; FL; RI; MA; - ; Jun; Dysentery;
    Sumter
CLARKE, J. J.; 6; M; White; NC; NC; NC; - ; Oct; Dysentery;
    Sumter
HAMMOND, R. S.; 4; F; White; PA; Ireland; Ireland; - ; Oct;
    Croup; Sumter
HAMMOND, Emma; 2; F; White; PA; Ireland; Ireland; - ; Nov;
    Diptheria; Sumter
ANDERSON, Jonathan; 1; M; White; FL; GA; AL; - ; Oct; Flux;
    Sumter
PLATT, Robt. L.; 1; M; White; FL; GA; AL; - ; Aug; Spasms;
    Sumter
SMITH, Jno. E.; 55; M; White; TN; - ; - ; Farmer; Aug; Asthma;
    Sumter
MARSH, Seaborn; 1; M; White; FL; GA; SC; - ; July; Congestion;
    Sumter
YOUNG, John; 3; M; White; SC; SC; SC; - ; Nov; Fever; Sumter
SWEARINGEN, J. H.; 59; M; White; SC; SC; SC; Farmer; June;
    Consumption; Sumter

BROOKS, Ethel F.; 2; F; White; AL; GA; GA; - ; Nov;
Dysentery; Sumter
BROOKS, Dasey; 1; F; White; FL; GA; GA; - ; Sept; Dysentery;
Sumter
BUTLER, Susan; 10; F; White; AL; GA; GA; - ; May; Inflam.
Bowels; Sumter
DeBUSKE, Lizzie; 1; F; White; FL; GA; GA; - ; Dec; Congestion;
Sumter
HODGES, Mamie; 32; F; White; GA; SC; SC; - ; Nov;
Consumption; Sumter
BELLAMY, Pearl; 6; F; White; SC; FL; SC; - ; July; Brain fever;
Sumter
WARNOCK, Jno S.; 24; M; White; GA; SC; GA; Farmer; Dec;
Yellow Fever; Sumter
WILKISON, Pearl; 1; F; White; FL; FL; GA; - ; Jan; Brain
affected; Sumter
HARRISON, P. U.; 32; F; White; GA; GA; GA; - ; Dec; Fever;
Sumter
CARRUTHERS, S. M.; 2; F; White; FL; FL; FL; - ; Oct; Bilious
Fever; Sumter
DIAS, Eddie; 1; F; White; FL; FL; SC; - ; Feb; Pneumonia;
Sumter
FORT, Harriet; 60; F; White; SC; SC; SC; - ; Nov; Consumption;
Sumter
COOK, W. E.; 17; M; White; GA; GA; GA; Laborer; July;
Typhoid Fever; Sumter
O'NEAL, E. J.; 26; F; White; GA; GA; GA; - ; Jan; Consumption;
Suwannee
OLIVER, Mary E.; 15; F; White; FL; GA; GA; - ; April; Malarial
Fever; Suwannee
POOSER, Ella; 30; F; White; VA; NC; VA; - ; March;
Pneumonia; Suwannee
LASSETER, A. V.; 35; F; White; SC; SC; SC; - ; March;
Pneumonia; Suwannee
SIMMONS, GeorgiAnna; 30; F; Black; FL; FL; FL; Housekeep;
June; Cong. Bowels; Suwannee
WOODS, Louisa; 21; F; White; FL; SC; SC; Housekeep; Dec;
Blood poison; Suwannee

Name; Age; Sex; Race; Born; FABorn; MOBorn;
        Occup; DODeath; Cause Of Death; County

NICKSON, Bryan; 70; M; Black; NC; - ; - ; Laborer; Oct; Cancer;
    Suwannee
KENNEDY, Hollon; 72; F; White; GA; GA; GA; Housekeep;
    June; Dropsey; Suwannee
BETHANY, Lucy; 45; F; Black; NC; NC; NC; Housekeep; June;
    Dropsey of heart; Suwannee
JACKSON, Silla; 4; F; Black; FL; GA; GA; - ; Feb; Burnt to
    death; Suwannee
McMANNA, Mary J.; 48; F; White; NC; NC; NC; Domestic; - ;
    Inflam. Bowels; Suwannee
LANE, Mary; 54; F; White; FL; GA; GA; Housekeep; May; - ;
    Suwannee
THRALLS, Esther; 70; F; White; IN; - ; - ; Housekeep; Nov;
    Dysentery; Suwannee
CLARK, Geo. W.; 7; M; White; FL; GA; FL; - ; Sept; Bilious
    Fever; Suwannee
AMONS, Sarah; 20; F; White; FL; - ; - ; - ; Oct; In Confinement;
    Suwanneé
BRYAN, W. B.; 57; M; White; FL; NC; NC; Farmer; Dec; Heart
    Disease; Suwannee
CHANCEY, Elizabeth; 20; F; White; - ; FL; - ; - ; July; Child
    Birth; Suwannee
JONES, Y.; 20; F; Black; GA; GA; GA; - ; May; Heart Disease;
    Suwannee
WARD, John W.; 2; M; White; FL; FL; FL; - ; June; Brain fever;
    Suwannee
HUNTER, M. C.; 18; F; White; FL; FL; TN; - ; July; Chill and
    fever; Suwannee
HUNTER, James; 12; M; White; FL; FL; TN; - ; June; Dropsey;
    Suwannee
KIRKLAND, H. K.; 58; M; White; GA; - ; - ; Farmer; June; Heart;
    Suwannee
McI(?), Ethel W.; 1; F; White; FL; GA; FL; - ; May; Whooping
    Cough; Suwannee
BARNETT, J. W.; 56; M; White; NC; NY; NC; Farmer; Dec;
    Heart Disease; Suwannee
GARDNER, J. L.; 67; M; White; IN; CT; PA; - ; Nov; Heart
    Dropsey; Suwannee

ROSS, H. E.; 2; F; White; FL; GA; FL; Minister; July; Liver Disease; Suwannee

BYNUM, J. A.; 55; M; White; GA; GA; GA; Lawyer; Oct; - ; Suwannee

CARROLL, Mrs. F.; 38; F; White; SC; FL; SC; Housekeep; Mar; Heart Disease; Suwannee

BRADDY, M. A.; 32; F; White; FA; GA; FL; Housekeep; Mar; - ; Suwannee

NOBLES, W. F.; 42; M; White; SC; SC; SC; Farmer; Dec; - ; Suwannee

MOLAND, H.; 24; F; Black; FL; SC; GA; Housekeep; June; - ; Suwannee

AILEN, W.; 14; M; Black; FL; SC; GA; Lawnwork; Mar; - ; Suwannee

JONES, M.; 38; F; Black; GA; GA; GA; Housekeep; Mar; Pneumonia; Suwannee

MATHIS, L.; 21; F; Black; FL; - ; - ; Laborer; Feb; Drowned; Suwannee

BROOKS, M.; 2; F; Black; FL; VA; SC; - ; Aug; Dropsey; Suwannee

WRIGHT, J.; 1; M; Black; FL; GA; FL; - ; Oct; Fits; Suwannee

WRIGHT, B.; 15; M; Black; SC; - ; - ; Lawnwork; Sept; - ; Suwannee

WRIGHT, N.; 60; F; Black; FL; - ; - ; Housekeep; Oct; Heart; Suwannee

JOHNSON, Clint; 73; M; Mu; GA; - ; GA; Lawnwork; July; Old Age; Suwannee

LILLY, E.; 24; F; White; FL; GA; - ; Lawnwork; June; - ; Suwannee

MEEKS, L.; 74; F; White; NC; NC; NC; Housekeep; Aug; Heart Affection; Suwannee

OHARA, C. L.; 74; M; White; PA; Ireland; PA; Shoemake; Apr; Asthma; Suwannee

PETERSON, D.; 22; F; Black; FL; VA; VA; Laborer; Oct; Consumption; Suwannee

HUNTER, M. L.; 1; M; Black; FL; - ; - ; - ; Sept; - ; Suwannee

PAGE, D.; 23; M; White; GA; VA; VA; Farmer; Feb; Pneumonia; Suwannee

PISON, Henry; 76; M; White; GA; SC; SC; Farmer; Mar; Asthma;
     Suwannee
CARRUTHERS, James; 80; M; Black; GA; GA; GA; Laborer;
     Feb; Unknown; Suwannee
CARROLL, J. D.; 25; M; White; FL; NC; NC; Farmer; Mar;
     Congestion; Suwannee
REDDING, W. H.; 1; M; White; FL; - ; SC; - ; July; - ; Suwannee
BYRD, W. H.; 27; M; White; FL; GA; GA; Mechanic; June; - ;
     Suwannee
NEVILS, O.; 2; M; White; SC; FL; SC; - ; July; - ; Suwannee
MARKS, Thomas; 36; M; Black; GA; - ; - ; Farmer; June; Killed;
     Suwannee
JOHNSON, Nannie; 1; F; White; FL; GA; SC; - ; Nov; Remittant
     fever; Suwannee
POTTER, J. L.; 3; M; White; VA; England; VA; - ; Sept; - ;
     Suwannee
POTTER, G. L.; 1; M; White; VA; England; VA; - ; Oct; Brain
     fever; Suwannee
PAPPELL, Ada; 18; F; White; FL; NC; SC; - ; Sept; Malarial
     Fever; Taylor
HEDGECOCK, John; 23; M; White; FL; - ; - ; Farmer; Mar;
     Congestion brain; Taylor
JENKINS, Ella; 26; F; White; FL; FL; NC; - ; Oct; Child Bed;
     Taylor
NEWBERN, Thos; 3; M; White; FL; GA; GA; - ; Sept; Unknown;
     Taylor
NEWBERN, Geo.; 2; M; White; FL; GA; GA; - ; Sept; Unknown;
     Taylor
BLANCHARD, Hattie; 88; F; White; NC; VA; VA; - ; Oct; Fall,
     cripple; Taylor
DEVANE, Mary; 1; F; White; FL; FL; FL; - ; Nov; Whooping
     Cough; Taylor
DEVANE, Laura; 1; F; White; FL; FL; FL; - ; Nov; Whooping
     Cough; Taylor
FIFE, Wm. S.; 35; M; White; FL; NC; NC; Farmer; Mar;
     Pneumonia; Taylor
MATTHIS, (none given); 1; M; White; FL; FL; FL; - ; Aug; Cold;
     Taylor

MATTHIS, (none given); 1; M; White; FL; FL; FL; - ; Aug; Cold; Taylor

KING, Dashy; 2; F; White; FL; NC; AL; - ; Sept; Burned; Taylor

GUTHERY, Wm.; 49; M; White; GA; SC; SC; Farmer; Mar; Pneumonia; Taylor

FOWLER, Cleo; 4; F; White; FL; GA; FL; - ; Jan; Heart Dropsey; Taylor

EVANS, Amantha; 27; F; White; GA; FL; - ; Laborer; Oct; Malarial Fever; Taylor

PRIDGEN, John; 64; M; White; FL; GA; GA; - ; Oct; Pneumonia; Taylor

PRIDGEN, Floyd; 8; M; White; FL; GA; FL; - ; July; Fever; Taylor

BLACK, James; 2; M; White; FL; GA; FL; - ; Nov; Fever; Taylor

FAULKNER, Jno; 26; M; White; FL; GA; FL; Farmer; Mar; Dropsey; Taylor

WRIGHT, Samuel; 29; M; Black; SC; - ; - ; Farmer; July; Disorder of liver; Taylor

CALMON, Nancy; 20; F; Black; FL; - ; - ; - ; June; Malarial Fever; Taylor

MCCALL, Etta; 1; F; White; FL; GA; - ; - ; Sept; Typhoid Fever; Taylor

CARLTON, Oliver; 1; M; White; FL; GA; - ; - ; Mar; Congestion brain; Taylor

PEACOCK, Mary; 30; F; White; FL; GA; GA; - ; Mar; Dropsey; Taylor

YOUNG, Michael; 40; M; White; GA; SC; SC; Farmer; Mar; Pneumonia; Taylor

BAILEY, Burrell; 58; M; White; - ; - ; - ; - ; - ; Pneumonia; Taylor

WILDER, Jeremiah; 33; M; White; FL; GA; PA; - ; Mar; Pneumonia; Taylor

WILDER, Emeline; 28; F; White; FL; GA; PA; - ; Aug; - ; Taylor

HOWARD, Martha; 1; F; White; FL; AL; AL; - ; June; Pneumonia; Taylor

CARMICHAEL, Sephronia; 55; F; White; GA; AL; AL; Farmer; Nov; Congestion brain; Taylor

BENNETT, Wm; 71; M; White; SC; NC; NC; Farmer; Mar; Dropsey; Taylor

Name; Age; Sex; Race; Born; FABorn; MOBorn;
        Occup; DODeath; Cause Of Death; County

HOWARD, Cordelia; 25; F; White; LA; GA; LA; - ; Sept;
    Congestive chills; Taylor
HOWARD, John W.; 1; M; White; FL; GA; LA; - ; Sept;
    Congestive chills; Taylor
HALE, Mary J.; 27; F; White; NC; SC; Nova Sco.; - ; Mar;
    Abscess of lungs; Taylor
HENRY, Ella V.; 1; F; White; FL; NC; FL; - ; Sept; Risen in head;
    Taylor
COKER, Steven; 22; M; White; FL; GA; FL; Laborer; May;
    Pneumonia; Taylor
HOLLAND, Mary; 29; F; White; FL; FL; AL; Sewing; Apr;
    Typhoid Fever; Taylor
DONALDSON, E. F.; 33; M; White; GA; GA; NC; Farmer; Apr;
    Pneumonia; Taylor
WHIDDEN, Dan C.; 1; M; White; FL; FL; FL; - ; Sept; Inflam.
    Bowels; Taylor
YOUNG, Tony A.; 4; M; White; FL; FL; FL; - ; Oct; - ; Taylor
SHEFFIELD, Bryan; 76; M; White; GA; GA; GA; Farmer; Mar;
    Pneumonia; Taylor
SAPP, William W.; 3; M; White; FL; FL; FL; - ; Oct; Fever;
    Taylor
REAMS, Jane; 2; F; White; FL; FL; FL; - ; July; Congestion
    brain; Taylor
SAPP, Morton; 17; M; White; FL; FL; FL; Farmer; July;
    Congestion brain; Taylor
WOODS, Mary; 15; F; White; AL; AL; AL; - ; Spet; Child birth;
    Taylor
CUKES, Luciana; 21; F; White; FL; TN; FL; - ; Jan; Dropsey;
    Taylor
YORK, Martha; 24; F; White; FL; TN; FL; - ; July; Brain fever;
    Taylor
SADDLES, Daniel; 4; M; White; FL; FL; FL; - ; July; Brain fever;
    Taylor
MASSEY, Dr.; 35; M; White; - ; - ; - ; - ; Dec; Consumption;
    Taylor
DePRATTER, Susan; 45; F; White; GA; GA; GA; - ; Dec; Fever;
    Volusia

ROBERTS, E. J.; 16; F; White; FL; GA; GA; - ; June; Fever;
Volusia

McCLAIN, Harriet; 44; F; White; SC; SC; SC; - ; Apr; Fever;
Volusia

McCLAIN, Julia A.; 14; F; White; FL; SC; SC; - ; Apr;
Pneumonia; Volusia

COZART, S. W.; 30; M; White; GA; GA; GA; - ; Oct; Shot;
Volusia

JACKSON, Fanny; 25; F; White; SC; SC; SC; - ; Oct; Congestive
chills; Volusia

SMITH, Walter; 13; M; White; OH; OH; OH; - ; Dec; Typhoid
Fever; Volusia

FLOYD, Geo; 2; M; White; GA; GA; GA; - ; Feb; Dis of mitral
valve; Volusia

DOHN, C. L.; 35; M; White; Sweden; Sweden; Sweden; - ; - ; - ;
Volusia

CLARK, L.; 5; F; Black; FL; FL; FL; - ; - ; Fever; Volusia

HARWOOD, N. D.; 55; M; White; MN; - ; - ; Planter; May; Cong
brain; Volusia

SHARP, Jas.; 25; M; Black; SC; - ; - ; Laborer; May; Venereal
Disease; Volusia

McBURNEY, Eliza; 5; F; Black; FL; SC; SC; - ; Jan; Chills and
fever; Volusia

ROSEBORO,Jacob; 40; M; Black; AL; AL; AL; Farmer; Oct;
Complication; Volusia

McLEAN, John; 28; M; White; CT; CT; CT; Livery; Apr;
Consumption; Volusia

McLEAN, C. S.; 32; M; White; CT; CT; CT; Clerk; Mar;
Consumption; Volusia

WILLIAMS, Wm.; 30; M; Black; SC; SC; SC; Farmer; June; Sun
Stroke; Volusia

LAKE, James; 18; M; Black; FL; FL; FL; Laboer; Jan;
Rheumatism; Volusia

FERGUSON, Julia; 64; F; Black; SC; SC; SC; - ; May;
Consumption; Volusia

JOHNSON, Jas.; 22; M; Black; FL; FL; GA; Laborer; Apr;
Murdered; Volusia

Name; Age; Sex; Race; Born; FABorn; MOBorn;
        Occup; DODeath; Cause Of Death; County

THOMAS, Alice; 7; F; Black; FL; SC; SC; - ; June; Cerebral
    spinal fev; Volusia
BUSHNELL, A. L.; 76; M; White; NY; NY; NY; Merchant; May;
    Congestive fever; Volusia
MARKS, Anthony; 48; M; Black; AL; AL; AL; Farmer; Dec;
    Poisoned; Volusia
MUSK, Amelia; 45; F; Black; AL; AL; AL; - ; May; - ; Volusia
McKINZAY, Ruford; 16; M; White; SC; SC; SC; - ; Aug; Scarlet
    Fever; Volusia
McKINZAY, Grace; 8; F; White; FL; FL; FL; - ; Aug; Scarlet
    Fever; Volusia
MCKINZAY, Nathan; 5; M; White; FL; FL; FL; - ; Aug; Scarlet
    Fever; Volusia
FREEMAN, John; 40; M; Black; SC; - ; - ; Laborer; Mary;
    Consumption; Volusia
HARDING, Joe; 30; M; White; NY; - ; - ; Clerk; Jan;
    Consumption; Volusia
BISHOP, Dr. (wife of); 30; F; White; NY; - ; - ; - ; Mar; Inflam.
    Bowels; Volusia
LEEK, Geo.; 30; M; White; NY; - ; - ; Carpenter; June;
    Consumption; Volusia
ZIEGLER, (none given); 23; - ; White; FL; GA; GA; - ; June; - ;
    Volusia
AUSTIN, John; 45; M; White; FL; IN; IN; - ; June; - ; Volusia
MONROE, Archie; 45; M; Black; SC; - ; - ; Laborer; June; - ;
    Volusia
JOHNSON, Bill; 6; M; Black; FL; - ; - ; - ; Aug; - ; Volusia
JEEMS, Randall; 7; M; Black; FL; - ; - ; - ; Aug; - ; Volusia
DUYER, Mrs.; 25; F; White; NY; - ; - ; - ; Aug; Consumption;
    Volusia
CANNING, J. S.; 30; M; White; MA; - ; - ; - ; Sept; Consumption;
    Volusia
SLAUGHT, Miss; 40; F; White; NY; - ; - ; - ; Oct; Consumption;
    Volusia
BINDER, Mrs. A.; 30; F; White; Hungary; Hungary; Hungary; - ;
    Oct; Consumption; Volusia
SLAUGHTER, (none given); 1; - ; White; FL; - ; - ; - ; Oct; - ;
    Volusia

TAYLOR, James; 3; M; Black; FL; - ; - ; - ; Dec; - ; Volusia

COLE, Jacob; 65; M; White; NY; - ; - ; - ; Jan; - ; Volusia

THOMAS, Annie; 30; F; White; KY; - ; - ; - ; May; - ; Volusia

HUGHES, Alice G.; 1; F; White; FL; AL; FL; - ; July; Bilious
Fever; Wakulla

HAM, David; 1; M; White; FL; FL; FL; - ; July; Bilious Fever;
Wakulla

McWILLIAMS, J. R.; 80; M; White; SC; SC; SC; Farmer; Nov;
Decrepid; Wakulla

RIVELL, Mary; 36; F; White; FL; - ; - ; - ; May; Dropsey;
Wakulla

RODDENBURY, Jane; 20; F; White; FL; NC; NC; - ; Aug;
Dropsey; Wakulla

HAM, David; 70; M; White; GA; GA; GA; Ferryman; May;
Apoplexy; Wakulla

ANDREWS, J. R.; 28; M; White; FL; GA; GA; Farmer; June;
Consumption; Wakulla

VICKERS, Rayford; 1; M; White; FL; FL; FL; - ; July; Bilious
fever; Wakulla

FITZGERALD, Nancy; 75; F; White; Ireland; Ireland; Ireland; - ;
Dec; Old Age; Wakulla

HALL, Celia; 58; F; Black; VA; VA; VA; - ; Oct; Effects of
burns; Wakulla

BAKER, Mary J.; 28; F; White; GA; GA; GA; - ; May; Child
birth; Wakulla

MATHERS, H. E.; 2; F; Black; FL; FL; FL; - ; July; - ; Wakulla

STEPHENS, Eliza; 37; F; White; AL; GA; GA; - ; Jan; - ;
Wakulla

DUGGER, Mariam; 75; F; White; NC; NC; NC; - ; Feb; General
old age; Wakulla

GREEN, F. T.; 63; M; White; SC; SC; SC; Farmer; Dec;
Apoplexy; Wakulla

GREEN, B. C.; 6; W; White; FL; SC; SC; - ; Sept; Enlarge gland;
Wakulla

GRAY, Martha; 1; F; White; FL; GA; GA; - ; June; - ; Wakulla

COX, Ada C.; 5; F; White; FL; GA; FL; - ; July; Inflam. Bowels;
Wakulla

Name; Age; Sex; Race; Born; FABorn; MOBorn;
Occup; DODeath; Cause Of Death; County

JOHNSON, Maria; 20; F; Black; FL; GA; GA; Farm work; Dec;
Dropsey of heart; Wakulla
HARGRETT, Fannie; 75; F; Black; NC; NC; NC; - ; Apr; - ;
Wakulla
LAIRD, B. F.; 62; M; White; GA; - ; - ; Farm work; Nov;
Pneumonia; Wakulla
JACKSON, Handy; 57; M; Black; - ; - ; - ; - ; Oct; - ; Wakulla
FERRELL, (none given); 1; M; White; AL; GA; FL; - ; Mar; - ;
Wakulla
MERCER, Rosanna; 36; F; Black; AL; - ; - ; Farm work; Nov;
Dropsey; Wakulla
BUTLER, Eviline; 53; F; White; GA; GA; GA; - ; Apr; - ;
Wakulla
ANDERSON, Mary E.; 27; F; White; FL; SC; GA; - ; Jan;
Consumption; Wakulla
POWELL, M. J.; 29; F; White; FL; SC; SC; - ; Arp; Inflam of
womb; Wakulla
PIGOTT, Mattie; 11; F; White; FL; SC; SC; - ; Mar; Heart
Disease; Wakulla
REYNOLDS, Nancy; 38; F; White; SC; SC; SC; - ; Apr;
Rheumatism; Wakulla
CRUM, Zilpha; 17; F; White; VA; VA; VA; - ; Dec; Dropsey;
Wakulla
HILL, (none given); 1; F; Black; FL; GA; AL; - ; July; - ; Wakulla
MILLER, Emmaline; 1; F; White; FL; FL; FL; - ; Mar; - ; Wakulla
BENTON, Mary J.; 40; F; White; SC; SC; SC; - ; Mar; - ; Wakulla
OLIVER, M. J.; 35; F; White; FL; SC; FL; - ; Nov; Pneumonia;
Wakulla
LEVY, John S.; 10; M; White; FL; FL; FL; - ; Mar; Typhoid
Fever; Wakulla
GILCHRIST, L. R.; 45; M; White; FL; SC; SC; - ; Nov; - ;
Wakulla
MEACHAM, Bill; 12; M; White; SC; AL; AL; - ; Apr; Dropsey;
Walton
MEACHAM, James; 15; M; White; SC; AL; AL; - ; Sept;
Dropsey of heart; Walton
STUBBS, Chas.; 37; M; White; AL; AL; AL; Machinest; Mar;
Consumption; Walton

CAWTHER, Lough; 47; M; White; FL; GA; GA; - ; Apr; Inflam of bowels; Walton

GRAY, J. D.; 1; M; White; FL; Scotland; FL; - ; May; Dentition; Walton

TAYLOR, Henry; 1; M; Black; FL; TN; NC; - ; Apr; Diarhea; Walton

CRAWFORD, Sarah; 34; F; White; FL; SC; SC; - ; July; Inflammation; Walton

McCASKELL, Finley; 46; M; White; FL; NC; AL; Machinest; May; General dropsey; Walton

CRAWFORD, Asa; 26; F; White; FL; NC; AL; - ; Mar; - ; Walton

GOMILLION, Mary; 80; F; White; AL; GA; GA; - ; Aug; Fever; Walton

ANDERSON, Jane; 21; F; White; AL; AL; Al; - ; May; Peritinitis; Walton

McLEAN, Flora; 72; F; White; NC; NC; NC; - ; Jan; - ; Walton

McLEOD, Max; 1; M; White; FL; FL; AL; - ; Aug; Inflam of bowels; Walton

MURPHROE, Dref; 32; M; White; AL; AL; AL; - ; Apr; Unknown; Walton

PATTEN, E.; 48; M; White; MS; MS; MS; - ; Jan; Unknown; Walton

REYDON, Benj.; 42; M; White; AL; AL; AL; - ; July; Unknown; Walton

McDANIEL, Christine; 22; F; White; FL; NC; NC; - ; May; Consumption; Walton

KING, Chas.; 20; M; White; FL; AL; AL; - ; Apr; Accidental; Walton

BESON, Jemina; 59; F; White; FL; NC; NC; - ; Feb; Unknown; Walton

WILLIAMS, Hiram E.; 1; M; White; FL; FL; FL; - ; Oct; Accident by horse; Washington

SKIPPER, E. M.; 2; M; White; FL; FL; AL; - ; Oct; - ; Washington

MILLER, John; 3; M; White; FL; FL; FL; - ; Oct; Burned; Washington

SKIPPER, Jas. A.; 7; M; White; FL; FL; GA; - ; Sept; Apoplexy & fever; Washington

Name; Age; Sex; Race; Born; FABorn; MOBorn;
        Occup; DODeath; Cause Of Death; County

SKIPPER, John E.; 32; M; White; FL; FL; FL; - ; Mar; Opium
    habit; Washington
McLEOD, Wm.; 26; M; White; FL; FL; FL; - ; Mar; Pneumonia;
    Washington
RILEY, Wm F.; 2; M; White; FL; FL; FL; - ; Oct; Swamp fever;
    Washington
PRIMUS, Jacobs; 70; M; Black; FL; NC; NC; - ; Mar; General
    debility; Washington
McMULLEN, Gehazu J.; 35; F; White; AL; AL; AL; - ; Sept;
    Heart Disease; Washington
REDDICK, James; 72; W; White; GA; SC; SC; Farmer; Oct;
    Vertigo; Washington
SCOTT, Elizabeth; 18; F; White; FL; AL; AL; - ; Dec; Labor;
    Washington
LINTON, Rebecca; 24; F; White; FL; AL; AL; - ; May; Labor;
    Washington
LINTON, Roxey; 6; F; White; FL; AL; AL; - ; June; Flux;
    Washington
PEARSON, Elizabeth; 65; F; White; GA; VA; SC; - ; Nov;
    Pneumonia; Washington
HITCHINGS, Lucy; 12; F; White; WI; N. B.; ME; - ; June;
    Typhoid Fever; Volusia
HITCHINGS, Louisa; 13; F; White; WI; N. B.; ME; - ; June;
    Typhoid Fever; Volusia
BIELHY, (none given); 1; - ; White; FL; - ; - ; - ; Sept; - ; Volusia
FALKER, (none given); 3; - ; White; FL; - ; - ; - ; Jan; - ; Volusia
JOHNSON, Annie; 1; F; Black; FL; GA; FL; - ; Oct; - ; Wakulla
HAYMAN, George; 5; M; White; FL; Bahamas; FL; - ; Mar;
    Meningitis; Monroe
EDWARDS, Jose; 70; M; Black; Cuba; Cuba; Cuba; Cigarmaker;
    Mar; Heart Disease; Monroe
CURRY, James; 25; M; Black; Bahamas; Bahamas; Bahamas;
    Laborer; Mar; Rapid Consump.; Monroe
GOMEZ, Clara; 1; F; White; FL; Cuba; Cuba; - ; Mar; Meningitis;
    Monroe
RODRIGUEZ, Juan; 28; M; White; Cuba; Cuba; Cuba;
    Cigarmaker; Mar; Consumption; Monroe

McDONALD, George J.; 58; M; White; Ireland; Ireland; Ireland;
Seaman; Mar; Heart Disease; Monroe
NAVIS, Teresa L.; 1; F; White; FL; Cuba; Cuba; - ; Mar; Cholera
Infection; Monroe
deALMA, Antonio; 50; M; White; Cuba; Cuba; Cuba; Tob. Strip;
Mar; Cerebral Apoplexy; Monroe
CUNNINGHAM, Samuel; 29; M; Black; Bahamas; Bahamas;
Bahamas; Carpenter; Mar; Plethesis Pul.; Monroe
BETANCOURT, Amelia; 1; F; White; FL; Cuba; Cuba; - ; Mar;
Tuberculosis; Monroe
NELSON, James; 1; M; Black; FL; - ; - ; - ; Mar; Lock jaw;
Monroe
MORROW, Robert; 2; M; Black; FL; - ; - ; - ; Mar; Typhoid
Pneumon.; Monroe
BARTLUM, Mary; 20; F; White; FL; - ; - ; - ; Mar; Consumption;
Monroe
MUSE, Loretta C.; 20; F; White; FL; - ; - ; - ; Mar; Consumption;
Monroe
VALAC, Amelia; 3; F; White; FL; Cuba; Cuba; - ; Mar;
Pneumonia; Monroe
STURBERT, George; 18; M; White; FL; - ; - ; - ; Mar;
Hydrocephalus; Monroe
DILLON, Infant Charles; 1; M; White; Key West; Key West; Key
West; - ; July; Marasmus; Monroe
ECASSI, Antonio; 1; M; White; Key West; Cuba; Cuba; - ; July ;
Convulsions; Monroe
BULMAN, Isaac; 31; M; Black; Key West; Key West; Key West;
Laborer; July; Gastritis; Monroe
LEDWITCH, Inf. Wm. F.; 3; M; White; Key West; New Jersy;
Key West; - ; July; Marasmus; Monroe
deALBINAS, Pablo; 1; M; White; Key West; Cuba; Cuba; - ; July;
(Unreadable); Monroe
PINDER, Maria; 85; F; White; England; England; England; - ;
July; Old Age; Monroe
BETHEL, Inf. Samuel; 1; M; White; Key West; Key West; Key
West; - ; July; Premature birth; Monroe
HAVER, Alicia; 1; F; White; Key West; Key West; Cuba; - ; July;
(Unreadable); Monroe

THOMPSON, Lillian; 3; F; White; Key West; Bahamas;
    Bahamas; - ; July; Meningitis; Monroe
LEON, Fidelia; 1; F; White; Key West; Cuba; Cuba; - ; July; - ;
    Monroe
TOLAVER, Lucia; 1; F; White; Key West; Spain; Spain; - ; July;
    Cholera Infection; Monroe
HANIBAL, James A.; 1; M; Black; Key West; Africa; Africa; - ;
    July; Cholera Infection; Monroe
DELGADO, Daniel; 30; M; White; Key West; Cuba; Cuba; - ;
    July; Tetanus Infection; Monroe
FLORA, Margareta; 42; F; White; Cuba; Cuba; Cuba; - ; July;
    Diptheria; Monroe
PERCEU, Leonora; 20; F; Black; Key West; Bahamas; Bahamas;
    - ; July; Consumption; Monroe
GONZALEZ, Clotilde V.; 19; F; White; Key West; Cuba; Cuba; -
    ; July; Pernicious Fever; Monroe
JOSEPH, Inf. Wm. N; - ; M; Black; Key West; Bahamas;
    Bahamas; - ; Sept; Still Born; Monroe
ALBURY, Wm.; 35; M; White; Key West; Bahamas; Bahamas;
    Seaman; Sept; Paralysis; Monroe
deTORIS, Juan; 52; M; White; Cuba; Cuba; Cuba; Cigarmaker;
    Sept; Consumption; Monroe
HALL, John J.; 28; M; White; N J; N J; N J; Farmer; Sept;
    Pernicious Fever; Monroe
HARDY, Child of Samuel; - ; M; Black; Key West; Bahamas;
    Bahamas; - ; Oct; Still Born; Monroe
WRIGHT, Henry; 1; M; Black; Key West; FL; FL; ; Oct;
    Marasmus; Monroe
LEON, Theodore; 1; M; White; Key West; Cuba ; Key West; - ;
    Oct; Teething; Monroe
BARTHUN, Mary E.; 9; F; White; Key West; Key West; Key
    West; - ; Oct; Whooping cough; Monroe
BUERRO, CONSTIND; 1; F; White; Key West; Cuba; Cuba; - ;
    Oct; Colitis; Monroe
deMISSIA, Juan C.; 78; F; White; Unreadab; Spain; Spain; Tob.
    Strip; Oct; Consumption; Monroe
WRIGHT, Louisa; 28; F; Black; Bahamas; Bahamas; Bahamas;
    Washerwom; Oct; Consumption; Monroe

GULLAN, Louisa; 7; F; White; Key West; Key West; Key West; - ; Oct; Sore throat; Monroe

KELLY, Elizabeth A.; 1; F; White; Key West; Key West; Bahamas; - ; Oct; Cholera Infection; Monroe

SARARIA, Brasarra; 1; F; White; Key West; Cuba; Cuba; - ; Oct; Still Born; Monroe

PALMER, Rachel; 1; F; White; Key West; Key West; Key West; - ; Oct; Tetanus Infection; Monroe

GUANCHE, Domingo; 5; M; White; Key West; Cuba; Cuba; - ; Oct; Whooping cough; Monroe

RAMIREZ, Andrew; 66; F; White; Cuba; Cuba; Cuba; Tob. Strip; Oct; Typhoid; Monroe

REMISSO, (unreadable); 1; M; White; Key West; Cuba; Cuba; - ; Oct; Enteritis; Monroe

RUIZ, Andres; 1; M; White; Key West; Cuba; Cuba; - ; Oct; - ; Monroe

MACHLEON, Emilio T.; 1; M; White; Cuba; Cuba; Cuba; - ; Oct; Chronic Colitis ; Monroe

SAUNDER, Sarah; 1; F; Black; Key West; Bahamas; Bahamas; - ; Nov; unreadable; Monroe

FINLAYSON, Joseph A.; 1; M; Black; Key West; Bahamas; FL; - ; Nov; Inanition; Monroe

PEACON, Edward; 3; F; White; Key West; FL; FL; - ; Nov; Pertussis; Monroe

MEDLIN, R. L.; 1; F; White; Key West; Bahamas; Bahamas; - ; Nov; Convulsions; Monroe

RODRIGUEZ, Geneva; 1; F; Black; Key West; Cuba; Cuba; - ; Nov; Pneumonia; Monroe

TIFT, Louise; 1; F; White; Key West; Bahamas; Bahamas; - ; Nov; Manasmus; Monroe

RODRIGUEZ, LUCIA; 1; F; White; Key West; Cuba; Cuba; - ; Nov; Pneumonia; Monroe

CLAIN, Amanda M.; 1; F; Black; Key West; Bahamas; Bahamas; - ; Nov; Enteritis; Monroe

GWYNN, Rosetta; 1; F; White; Key West; Key West; Key West; - ; Nov; Pertussis; Monroe

MOOR, Thomas; 48; M; White; England; England; England; Seaman; Nov; Malarial Fever; Monroe

Name; Age; Sex; Race; Born; FABorn; MOBorn;
Occup; DODeath; Cause Of Death; County

TONIS, Juan; 52; M; White; Cuba; Cuba; Cuba; Cigarmaker;
Nov; Paralysis/bladder; Monroe

SAWYER, Charity; 1; F; Black; Key West; Bahamas; Bahamas; -
; Nov; Lock jaw; Monroe

ROBERTS, William; 1; M; Black; Key West; Bahamas; Bahamas;
- ; Nov; - ;

SANCHEZ, Joseph; 1; M; White; Key West; Cuba; Cuba; - ; Nov;
Accident; Monroe

CURRY, Esperanta; 1; F; White; Bahamas; Key West; Key West;
- ; Nov; Teething; Monroe

BOYER, Jennie; 1; F; White; Key West; Key West; Key West; - ;
Nov; Gastro?; Monroe

ABALL, Adeline Horn; 1; F; White; Key West; Cuba; Cuba; - ;
Nov; Tetanus Infection; Monroe

PAREDEA, Eugenio; 2; M; Black; Key West; Cuba; Cuba; - ;
Nov; Eclampsia; Monroe

ALMIDA, Minnie L.; 1; F; White; Key West; Spain; Spain; - ;
Dec; Lock Jaw; Monroe

PITA, Elvira; 2; F; White; Cuba; Cuba; Cuba; - ; Dec; Epilepsia;
Monroe

CANO, Asandia; 5; F; White; Key West; Spain; Spain; - ; Dec;
Pneumonia; Monroe

JOHNSON, El(unreadable); 6; F; Black; Key West; - ; - ; - ; Dec;
Lock Jaw; Monroe

FRIADO, Santiago; 50; M; White; Cuba; Cuba; Cuba;
Cigarmaker; Dec; Consumption; Monroe

ACHERSON, Grace; 3; F; White; Key West; Bahamas; Bahamas;
- ; Dec; Pneumonia; Monroe

RUSSELL, Justine; 1; F; Black; Key West; Bahamas; Bahamas; -
; Dec; Meningitis; Monroe

ROBERTS, Lottie; 6; F; White; Key West; Key West; Key West; -
; Dec; - ; Monroe

HERNANDEZ, Amboria M.; 68; F; White; Cuba; Cuba; Cuba; - ;
Dec; Acute Phthisis; Monroe

BORDERS, Munnia; 1; F; White; Key West; Cuba; Cuba; - ; Dec;
Inanition; Monroe

ABRIETGOE, Leocardeno; 1; M; White; Key West; Spain; Spain;
- ; Dec; Accident; Monroe

St. JOHN, Mary; 2; F; Black; Key West; Spain; Spain; - ; Dec;
Pertussis; Monroe
ARTOTZAGO, William; 1; M; White; Key West; Key West; Key
West; - ; Dec; Pertussis; Monroe
POZA, Rosa; 1; F; White; Cuba; Cuba; Cuba; - ; Dec; Cerebral
Fever; Monroe
ROSALES, Nicholas; 27; M; Black; Cuba; Cuba; Cuba; - ; Dec;
Heart Disease; Monroe
CAVALRY, Poncho; 1; F; Black; Key West; Bahamas; Bahamas;
- ; Dec; - ; Monroe
RUSSELL, Mary; 26; F; Black; Bahamas; Bahamas; Bahamas; - ;
Dec; Phthisis; Monroe
AURTIA, Mary; 24; F; Black; Key West; Africa; Africa; Cigar
Sel.; June; Heart Disease; Monroe
deSILVA, Josefa Burress; 24; F; White; Cuba; Cuba; Cuba; Tob.
Strip; June; Hydrocephalus; Monroe
DELSA, Louis; 1; F; Black; Key West; Africa; Africa; - ; June;
Lock Jaw; Monroe
PITCHER, Wm A.; 79; M; White; New York; America; America;
Merchant; June; Paralysis; Monroe
REYNA, Ampara; 1; F; White; Cuba; Cuba; Cuba; - ; June;
Enteritis; Monroe
LOWE, Danger; 40; M; Black; Bahamas; Africa; Africa; Seaman;
June; Abcess of Kidney; Monroe
ALLUESY, Avery; 1; F; White; Key West; Bahamas; Bahamas; -
; June; Convulsions; Monroe
AMES, Hamilton; 1; M; White; Key West; England; England; - ;
June; Marasmus; Monroe
CAREY, Ann E.; 1; F; White; Key West; England; England; - ;
June; Dysentery; Monroe
REED, Cornelia; 28; F; White; Key West; Bahamas; Bahamas; - ;
June; Enterio Fever; Monroe
MUELTON, William; 28; M; Black; Key West; Africa; Africa;
Laborer; June; Congestion lung; Monroe
CORNISH, James; 1; M; Black; Key West; Africa; Africa; - ;
June; Convulsions; Monroe
CORDERO, Joseph N.; 3; M; White; Key West; Cuba; Cuba; - ;
June; Cholera Infection; Monroe

Name; Age; Sex; Race; Born; FABorn; MOBorn;
              Occup; DODeath; Cause Of Death; County

INGRAHAM, Cathernise; 36; F; White; Bahamas; Bahamas;
    Bahamas; - ; June; Per. Fever; Monroe
RECIO, Jose; 38; M; Black; Cuba; Cuba; Cuba; Cigarmaker; June;
    Hanging; Monroe
OLHAM, John; 40; M; White; Norway; Norway; Norway;
    Seaman; June; Phthisis; Monroe
BAILEY, Child Sarah; - ; - ; White; Key West; Bahamas;
    Bahamas; - ; June; Still Born; Monroe
GRANARAS, Enrique G.; 1; M; White; Key West; Spain; Spain; -
    ; June; Congested brain; Monroe
ROMAGUERS, Nestor F.; 1; M; White; Key West; Cuba; Cuba; -
    ; June; Tetanus infantile; Monroe
VALDES, Elvida; 1; F; Black; Key West; Cuba; Cuba; - ; June;
    Cholera Infection; Monroe
SPATCHES, William; 1; M; Black; Key West; Bahamas;
    Bahamas; - ; June; Marasmus; Monroe
HANLEY, Fennish; 1; M; Black; Key West; Bahamas; Bahamas; -
    ; June; Convulsions; Monroe
GRIFFIN, Lillian C.; 1; F; White; Key West; Bahamas; Bahamas;
    - ; June; Marasmus; Monroe
VILyAGUERO, Luisa; 25; F; Black; Key West; Bahamas;
    Bahamas; Tob. Strip; June; Tepsis?; Monroe
WILSON, Laura; 1; F; Black; Key West; Bahamas; Bahamas; - ;
    June; Convulsions; Monroe
FERGUSON, Geo. W.; 72; M; White; N. J.; America; U. S.;
    Merchant; June; Syncope; Monroe
ALRASZ, William; 35; M; White; Key West; ?; ?; - ; June;
    Intersceptia; Monroe
ROBERTS, Samuel; 35; M; Black; Bahamas; Bahamas; Bahamas;
    Seaman; June; Cholera Morbus; Monroe
CASH, Rebecca; 33; F; White; Bahamas; England; England; Tob.
    Strip; June; Paritinitis?; Monroe
McDONALD, Joseph E.; 1; M; White; Key West; U.S.; U.S.; - ;
    June; Cholera Infantile; Monroe
ALVARZ, Dionisia; 1; F; White; Key West; Cuba; Cuba; - ; June;
    Remittent fever; Monroe
PASTAR, Mary P.; 78; F; White; Cuba; Cuba; Cuba;
    Washerwom; June; Apoplexy; Monroe

CUBESA, Francisco M.; 39; M; White; Key West; Spain; Spain;
Cigarmaker; June; Eneritis; Monroe
PICASO, Mercedes; 19; F; White; Cuba; Cuba; Cuba; Tob. Strip;
July; Typhoid Fever; Monroe
GURETTED, Infant John; - ; M; White; Cuba; Cuba; Cuba; - ;
July; Still Born; Monroe
RODGERS, Elizabeth; 42; F; White; Key West; Africa; Africa; - ;
July; Cancer of Womb; Monroe
RUSSELL, William; 1; M; White; FL; FL; FL; - ; Mar; Whooping
cough; Monroe
WALKER, Audrey V.; 2; F; White; FL; FL; FL; - ; June; Measles;
Monroe
BABCOCK, John C.; - ; M; White; MA; MA; MA; - ; Mar; Snake
Bite; Monroe
JERNIGAN, Callie; 9; F; White; FL; FL; FL; - ; Nov; Cong. Of
brain; Monroe
HARKES, Caroline E.; 41; F; White; FL; FL; FL; - ; Apr; Heart
Disease; Monroe
OLIVER, Daisy; 1; F; White; FL; AR; TN; - ; May; Measles;
Monroe
FLINT, Monroe; 2; M; White; FL; GA; GA; - ; Jan; Pneumonia;
Monroe
HENDRY, Lewis; 2; M; White; FL; FL; FL; - ; Oct; Spasms;
Monroe
ANDESON, R. C.; 65; M; White; VA; VA; VA; - ; Oct; Paralysis;
Monroe
WILSA, Caroline G.; 1; F; White; FL; GA; FL; - ; Oct; (none);
Monroe
McKINLEY, Elizabeth; 36; F; White; GA; FL; FL; - ; Jan;
Hemmorage kidne; Monroe
JONES, LeRoy; 23; M; White; SC; SC; SC; - ; Oct; Consumption;
Monroe
GALWAITH, Daniel; 60; M; White; SC; SC; SC; - ; Mar;
Drowning; Monroe
SANDS, Elizabeth; 25; F; M; FL; FL; FL; - ; June; Consumption;
Monroe
KELLUM, Thom.; 46; F; M; OH; OH; OH; - ; Nov; Fever;
Monroe

Name; Age; Sex; Race; Born; FABorn; MOBorn;
            Occup; DODeath; Cause Of Death; County

THOMAS, Isaac; 28; M; Black; FL; FL; FL; - ; Nov; Hemmorage
    kidne; Monroe
ACOSTA, Verassiso; 1; F; Black; Key West; Cuba; Cuba; - ;
    May; Convulsions; Monroe
WAITE, Flopey (or Flossy); 1; F; White; Key West; GA; FL; - ;
    May; Convulsions; Monroe
FINILLO, Vidennia; 1; F; Black; Key West; Cuba; Cuba; - ; May;
    Acute Meningitis; Monroe
JOHNSON, Sam W.; 51; M; White; Bahamas; Bahamas;
    Bahamas; - ; May; Paralysis; Monroe
WHALTON, Felicia; 90; F; White; FL; FL; FL; - ; May; Senile
    Decay; Monroe
LINES, Charles; 4; M; Black; Key West; Key West; Key West; - ;
    July; Marasmus; Monroe
COOPER, George; 28; M; Black; Key West; FL; FL; Laborer;
    Aug; Consumption; Monroe
TULLY, George E.; 54; M; Black; Bahamas; Bahamas; Bahamas;
    Laborer; Aug; Consumption; Monroe
OLUDELL, Diego; 28; M; White; Cuba; Cuba; Cuba;
    Cigarmaker; Aug; Tiper's Pulmmales; Monroe
WILLIAMS, Sophia H.; 1; F; White; Key West; Bahamas;
    Bahamas; - ; Aug; Cholera; Monroe
HUMBOLT, Annie; 54; F; Black; Bahamas; A; A; Washerwom;
    Aug; Consumption; Monroe
CURRY, Augusta N.; 1; F; Black; Key West; - ; - ; - ; Aug;
    Pneumonia; Monroe
URIOLA, Rafael; 1; M; Black; Key West; Cuba; Cuba; - ; Aug;
    Tetano Infantile; Monroe
GUILLO, Vernacio; 3; M; Black; Key West; Cuba; Cuba; - ; Aug;
    (Unreadable); Monroe
VALDEZ, Gregorio; 4; M; Black; Key West; Cuba; Cuba; - ; Aug;
    Tetanus Infantile; Monroe
de Los OPELLO, Maria; 1; F; White; Key West; Cuba; Cuba; - ;
    Aug; Tetanus Infantile ; Monroe
JOHNSON, Mary E.; 1; F; White; Key West; Cuba; Cuba; - ; Aug;
    Inanition; Monroe
JORGE, Perfecta Diaz; 36; F; White; Cuba; Cuba; Cuba; Tob.
    Strip; Aug; Stomach Cancer; Monroe

WELLS, Catherine; 1; F; White; Key West; Bahamas; Bahamas; -
; Aug; Diarrhea; Monroe
ORTIZ, Manuela; 52; F; White; Cuba; Cuba; Cuba; Tob. Strip;
Aug; Parabida; Monroe
BOCKER, Daniel; 40; M; White; Bahamas; Bahamas; Bahamas;
Laborer; Aug; (unreadable); Monroe
UGARTE, Petronia; 1; F; White; Key West; Cuba; Cuba; - ; Aug;
Teething; Monroe
ROBERTS, John N.; 57; M; White; Bahamas; Bahamas;
Bahamas; Seaman; Aug; Lipsis Pulmmelu; Monroe
LAURES, Jose; 23; M; Black; Cuba; Cuba; Cuba; Cigarmaker;
Aug; Drowned; Monroe
SHEPARD, Lillian; 4; F; White; NM; NM; NM; - ; Aug;
Peritinitis; Monroe
ALLMY, Henry; 1; M; White; Key West; Bahamas; Bahamas; - ;
Aug; Cholera; Monroe
SWEETING, John M.; 1; M; White; Key West; - ; - ; - ; Aug;
Cholera; Monroe
ESQUIMALDO, Anna B.; 1; F; White; Key West; Cuba; Cuba; - ;
Aug; Pernicious Fever; Monroe
McCALE, James; 1; F; M; - ; Key West; - ; - ; Aug; Convulsions;
Monroe
LOPEZ, Rufina; 39; F; White; Cuba; Cuba; Bahamas; Tob. Strip;
Aug; Phthisis Pulmon.; Monroe
GUITERAS, Lewis; 1; M; White; Key West; Cuba; Cuba; - ; Aug;
? Parturetion; Monroe
DAVIS, Deania; 19; F; Black; Bahamas; Bahamas; Bahamas;
Washerwom; Aug; Chronic Dysentery; Monroe
BENIGUOCRUZ, George; 1; M; White; Key West; Cuba; Cuba; -
; Aug; Configuma; Monroe
ACINTERO, Felipe; 66; M; White; Cuba; Cuba; Cuba;
Cigarmaker; Sept; (Unreadable); Monroe
HARRIS, William; 103; M; White; Bahamas; Bahamas; Bahamas;
- ; Sept; Hypertrophy Heart; Monroe
MENZ, Manuel; 50; M; White; Cuba; Spain; Spain; Cigarmaker;
Sept; Old Age; Monroe
WRIGHT, Alexander; 3; M; Black; Key West; Bahamas;
Bahamas; - ; Sept; Phthsis Pulmon.; Monroe

MORROW, Robert; 1; M; White; Key West; - ; - ; - ; Sept;
Enteritis; Monroe

CURRY, Gertrude; 1; F; Black; Key West; - ; - ; - ; Sept; Lock
Jaw; Monroe

ADAMS, Frank; 1; M; Black; Key West; - ; - ; - ; Sept; Lock Jaw;
Monroe

RODRIGUEZ, Nicholas B.; 2; M; White; NY; Cuba; Cuba; - ;
Sept; - ; Monroe

HARDLY, Calvin S.; 36; F; White; Bahamas; Bahamas; Bahamas;
- ; Mar; Dropsey; Monroe

BETHEL, W. Lord; 1; F; White; Key West; Bahamas; Bahamas; -
; Apr; Typhoid Fever; Monroe

GORGES, Jesus; 52; M; White; Cuba; Cuba; Cuba; Cigarmaker;
Apr; Phthsis ; Monroe

GIBSON, Delia; 1; F; White; Bahamas; Bahamas; Bahamas; - ;
Apr; Membrane Cong.; Monroe

JONNS, Richard; 24; M; White; Bahamas; Bahamas; Bahamas;
Seaman; Apr; Bright's Disease; Monroe

WALLACE, Margaret; 24; F; Black; Bahamas; Bahamas;
Bahamas; Washerwom; Apr; Phthsis; Monroe

CUNNINGHAM, Samuel; 1; M; Black; Key West; Bahamas;
Bahamas; - ; Apr; Comp.; Monroe

CRYBELO, Juliana; 73; F; White; Cuba; Cuba; Cuba; Tob. Strip;
Apr; Bright's Disease; Monroe

WALTERS, Henrietta; 6; F; Black; Key West; Bahamas;
Bahamas; - ; Apr; Dysentery; Monroe

WALTCUM, Laura E.; 4; F; White; FL; FL; FL; - ; Apr; Typhoid
Fever; Monroe

GERGER, John H.; 78; M; White; FL; PA; PA; - ; Apr;
Pneumonia; Monroe

KNOWLES, Wm. Israel; 1; M; White; Key West; Key West; Key
West; - ; Apr; Pneumonia; Monroe

GANZALES, Elurtens; 1; M; Black; Key West; Cuba; Cuba; - ;
Apr; Cholera; Monroe

TIFT, Mary; 1; F; White; Key West; Bahamas; Bahamas; - ; Apr;
Pneumonia; Monroe

TRAN, Ejaos; 1; M; White; Key West; Cuba; Cuba; - ; Apr;
Inaition; Monroe

BARNE, Florence; 1; F; Black; Key West; Bahamas; Bahamas; - ;
Apr; Marasmus; Monroe
TOSSIS, Fernando; 75; F; White; Cuba; Cuba; Cuba; Cigarmaker;
Apr; Trisima Mono; Monroe
RODRIGUEZ, Mary; 8; F; White; Cuba; Cuba; Cuba; - ; May;
Liver complaint; Monroe
CAMBRIDGE, Mabel; 1; F; Black; Key West; Bahamas;
Bahamas; - ; May; Aneurism heart; Monroe
KNOWLES, Oscar; 41; M; White; Bahamas; Bahamas; Bahamas;
Seaman; May; Marasmus; Monroe
HARYS(HARRIS?), Franciso; 1; M; Black; Key West; Cuba;
Cuba; - ; May; Congestion brain; Monroe
CUBA, Patrico; 1; M; Black; Key West; Cuba; Cuba; - ; May;
Acute Meningitis; Monroe
YUCLID(?), Gumaconds; 1; M; Black; Key West; Cuba; Cuba; - ;
May; Cholera; Monroe
CANTURAS, Guero; 62; M; White; Cuba; Cuba; Cuba;
Cigarmaker; May; Meningitis; Monroe
ARMES, Waldo; 1; M; White; Key West; Cuba; Cuba; - ; May;
Meningitis; Monroe
WALLACE, Lillian; 1; F; Black; Key West; FL; FL; - ; May;
Spinal Meningitis; Monroe
GUERA, Bienvenido; 1; M; White; Key West; Cuba; Cuba; - ;
May; Cholera; Monroe
MERIDES, Manuel; 73; M; M; Cuba; Cuba; Cuba; Cigarmaker;
May; Senile Decay; Monroe
TEMP, Eliza M.; - ; F; White; Key West; Bahamas; Bahamas; - ;
May; Meningitis; Monroe
PAPY, Joseph; 1; M; White; Key West; FL; Bahamas; - ; May;
Marasmus; Monroe
PEREZ, Josefa Cordova; 21; F; White; Cuba; Cuba; Cuba; - ;
May; Heart Disease; Monroe
HENRIGUEZ, Augustino; 1; F; White; Key West; Cuba; Cuba; - ;
May; Tetanus Infantile; Monroe
KEMP, Charity; 80; F; White; Bahamas; Bahamas; Bahamas; - ;
May; Consumption; Monroe
ALVARADO, Mary; 1; F; White; Bahamas; Bahamas; Bahamas; -
; May; Meningitis; Monroe

124   Name; Age; Sex; Race; Born; FABorn; MOBorn;
               Occup; DODeath; Cause Of Death; County

HERNANDEZ, Manuel; 23; M; M; Cuba; Cuba; Cuba;
    Cigarmaker; May; Consumption; Monroe
FANGUI, Cuelio; - ; - ; - ; Cuba; Cuba; Cuba; Cigarmaker; May;
    Bright's Disease; Monroe
SYMMETT, Patience; 31; F; Black; Bahamas; Bahamas;
    Bahamas; Washerwom; May; Consumption; Monroe

Index

2

Index

Olone, 76
Samuel, 113
Teresa, 7
W. Lord, 122
Bethewsher
H. A. (?), 20
Betsic, 28
Beville
Josephine, 97
Beyard
James, 78
Bias
Samuel, 80
Bielhy, 112
Binder
Mrs. A., 108
Bishop
Dr.(wife of), 108
Black, 43
James, 105
Jessie, 88
Blackmon
Ellison, 39
Blackwell
Noah, 22
Blair
Montgomery, 100
Blake
F. B., 64
H. L., 64
I. I., 64
Blanchard
Hattie, 104
Blanton
A. T., 82
Blocker
Jeffrey, 63
Bloom
L. A., 84
Blount
H., 29
Blunt, 43
Boatwright
J. L, 52
Mary, 52
Bocker

Daniel, 121
Boden
Lottie, 5
Bogbrick
F., 91
Bohannon
Cornelia, 91
Bond
Rosina, 86
Boone
A. I. V., 42
Boork
John, 22
Boourquardez
Louisa, 36
Borders
Munnia, 116
Bosworth
Frances L., 85
Bourquardz
Constance, 36
Bowers
Corcket, 39
Boyd
A. M., 11
Allice, 11
Clara, 47
Boyer
Jennie, 116
Boykin
Reddie, 59
Rhoda, 59
Boyt
R. R., 73
Bracy
M. E., 84
Braddy
M. A., 103
Bradford
Jos. T., 95
Bradwell, 29
Bramlet
Thos, 46
Bramlett
Misouri, 52
Branch

Ira, 88
Braxton
Corbin, 26
Bray
Benj., 92
Breman
J., 31
Brennan
Edw., 4
Florenca, 4
James, 4
Brickell
Elsworth, 88
Brickhammer
Mary, 68
Bridges
B. F., 60
Brinson
Ann, 62
Mary, 62
Brit
Thomas, 21
Brita
(Child), 78
Britt
J. C., 82
Brockway
Lewis, 77
Brogden
Ada, 42
Bronson
Henrietta, 81
Brookins
Ben, 45
Brooks
Ansy, 6
Dasey, 101
Ethel F., 101
Lot, 45
M., 103
Rachel, 46
Brown
Ellen, 12
Emilio, 78
Emma, 23
Green, 34

3

Index

Index

Ann E., 117
Carley
  J., 57
Carlisle
  W. W., 46
Carlton
  Florence, 71
  Mable, 71
  Oliver, 105
Carmichael
  Sephronia, 105
Carmichail
  M, 15
Carr
  Davy, 91
Carraway
  H. M., 66
Carroll
  J. D., 104
  Mrs. F., 103
  Press, 89
Carruthers
  D. H., 84
  James, 104
  S. M., 101
Carter
  Alice May, 95
  J., 57
Cary
  Infant, 77
Casady
  J. W., 46
Casey
  Char, 74
  Kate, 13
  Naomi, 99
Cash
  Rebecca, 118
Cason
  W. H., 7
  Wallace, 66
Casson
  Clorida, 93
Castle
  Mary F., 11
Castrine

Mandy, 85
Castro
  Filipe, 77
Cavalry
  Poncho, 117
Cawther
  Lough, 111
Chairs
  Douglas, 53
  Green, 53
Chalmers
  E., 6
Chambers
  George, 5
  Mrs. Cassie, 1
Chancey
  Elizabeth, 102
Chandler
  John, 52
  Rosetta, 26
Chappell
  Gracie, 3
Chapple
  A. G., 10
Chapuro
  Jo., 76
Charles
  Jms., 59
Chase
  Lillie, 86
Chatton
  Easton, 80
Chavez
  Esteban, 74
Child
  J. N., 99
Childers
  Chas., 96
China
  G. G., 3
Christmas
  Alice, 50
Christopher
  Ann, 45
Clain
  Amanda M., 115

Clark
  Charles, 87
  Charlotte, 6
  Geo. W., 102
  James K., 88
  L., 107
  Mary, 34
  Mrs. J. L., 23
  Wm., 15
Clarke
  Baby, 19
  Isaac, 19
  J. J., 100
Clay
  Selane, 36
Clear
  Sally, 48
Clem
  Hilliard, 28
Clemens
  Dolls, 68
Clemmons
  J. J., 39
Clifford
  Daisy, 19
Cobb
  Lena A, 1
  Milton, 45
Coffee
  Julia, 66
  Lancaster, 70
  Mary, 66
  Sallie, 69
  Wiley, 66
Cofield
  Victoria, 54
Coker
  Steven, 106
Colanell
  E. D., 23
Cole
  C. V., 59
  Jacob, 109
  Mary Ann, 21
Colebrook
  Frank, 76

5

Index

Index

Daniel
  E. C. J., 3
  Robt., 63
Daniels
  Jn., 56
Dantzler
  James, 54
Dasher
  Benj., 61
Daughtry
  M., 74
David
  Anna, 72
Davies
  Wm., 95
Davis
  Albert, 11
  Alice U., 36
  Cornelius, 68
  Deania, 121
  Dock, 14
  H. M., 82
  John, 21
  Margaret, 15
  Pat, 48
  Robt, 69
Dawsey
  Mollie, 72
Dawson
  Viola, 41
DeAlbinas
  Pablo, 113
DeAlma
  Antonio, 113
Dean
  John, 63
Dear
  Alfred, 7
DeBuske
  Lizzie, 101
DeCheniva
  Amanda, 38
Decorcis
  Mimi, 53
Deek
  Wm. S., 82

Dees
  A., 31
DeHaw
  Maud, 97
DeLaRus
  Henry, 16
DeLaughter
  Frances, 65
Delgado
  Daniel, 114
DeLosOpello
  Maria, 120
Delsa
  Louis, 117
Demare
  Infant, 57
DeMissia
  Juan C., 114
Dempsey
  Margaret, 31
Dene(unreadable)
  H, 32
Dennis
  Ellen, 58
  Infant, 41
Dent
  Julia, 51
DePew
  Infant, 36
DePratter
  Susan, 106
DeSilva
  Josefa Burress, 117
DeToris
  Juan, 114
Devane
  Laura, 104
  Mary, 104
DeVaughn
  Eliz., 81
Dewey
  John T., 35
Dias
  Eddie, 101
Dice
  Emery, 64

Dickson
  Joe, 8
Dillon
  Charles (infant), 113
Dismmukes
  Jns., 25
Dix
  Daniel, 10
Dixon
  Ben, 70
  H., 28
  M. E., 38
  Rosa, 70
Dohn
  C. L., 107
Donaldson
  E. F., 106
  Emma, 47
Donnelly
  Sarah, 82
Dooley
  Sarah, 40
Dorsey
  John Wesley, 49
  Starling, 49
Dossing
  F., 7
Douglas
  A. A., 97
  Cora, 2
  Jane, 82
  Mary, 17
  Victoria, 2
Douglass
  John, 64
  Nelly, 64
Dowling
  Clarence, 14
  David, 14
Doyle
  I., 74
Drigger
  Martha, 1
Druggors
  E., 84
Dubart

7

Index

James, 55
Dubois
  Louis P., 10
Duckworth
  J. F., 61
  Rosa, 61
  Van, 86
Duggan
  Eli, 58
Dugger
  Mariam, 109
Duncan
  Jennie, 99
Dunham
  Cassie, 88
Duprey
  A., 74
  P. J., 74
Dupuis
  D. S., 72
Duval
  Sallie, 66
Duyer
  Mrs., 108
Dwason
  M., 20
Dykes
  G. P., 84

E

Earle
  Sis, 61
Eason
  Bing, 58
Eastman
  H. C., 96, 98
Easton
  Chas. P., 94
Ecassi
  Antonio, 113
Eckteberger
  John, 23
Eddins
  Rebecca, 22
Edgar
  Dan'l., 94

Edgars
  Jms., 92
Edmund
  Frank, 19
Edward
  Mrs. I. T., 94
Edwards
  Ivan, 1
  Jose, 112
  Patty J., 42
  Richard, 31
  Wm., 80
  L., 13
Ellerbee
  J. N., 38
Elmore
  Ed, 67
English
  Mary, 13
  Rehina, 5
Enterkin
  Jas., 21
Eppes
  Henrietta, 25
Erwin
  Hatti, 36
Esquimaldo
  Anna B., 121
Esquivel
  Benj., 79
Etheridge
  Jno., 66
Evans
  Amanda, 83
  Amantha, 105
  Henrietta, 14
  Robert, 49
  Steven, 29
  William J., 88
Everett
  Henry, 85

F

Fairbanks
  Andrews, 51
Fairby

Blossie, 8
Falker, 112
Fannin
  C. B., 37
Fanqui
  Cuelio, 124
Farmer
  Jas., 11, 13
Faulk
  A., 92
Faulkner
  Jno, 105
Fendon
  D., 34
Fendwick
  Ed., 8
Fennell
  Bryant, 35
  Julia, 35
Fergeson
  Julia, 28
Ferguson
  Geo. W., 118
  Julia, 107
Fernald
  L. M., 85
Fernandez
  E. L., 10
Ferrell, 110
  M., 7
Ferriea
  Eugenia, 10
Ferris
  Henry, 35
Fields
  Wm., 57
Fife
  Wm. S., 104
Fillyace
  Amy, 28
Finillo
  Vidennia, 120
Finlayson
  Joseph A., 115
Finley
  Lizzie, 49

Index

Index

Index

11

Index

Hayman
George, 112
Haynes
C. T., 46
Hayrick
Gulleye, 64
Hays
Wm. R., 60
Hayward
James, 31
Hazen
A. E., 38
Hedgecock
John, 104
Helker
Cerena, 16
Hemps
M. E. E., 10
Henderson
D. M., 32
H. E., 6
Hendricks
Daniel, 58
Hendry
Emma, 71
Lewis, 119
Henosa
Clotilde, 74
Henriguez
Augustino, 123
Henry
Davy, 48
Ella V., 106
Geo., 69
Wm.., 46
Herera
Providencia, 74
Hernandez
Amboria M., 116
H., 19
Manuel, 124
Herndon
baby, 49
Mrs., 71
Hewett
Elizabeth, 39

Hewitt
Nelson, 42
Hicks
Eliza, 1
Henrietta, 78
Higginbotham
Elizabeth, 9
Higgins
Louisa, 45
Higgs
Infant (of Sophia Higgs), 78
High
L. T., 22
Hightower
Jesse, 45
Hill, 110
Etta, 14
Geo. W., 83
Jno, 10
John, 61
R. L., 23
Richard, 51
Scinda, 47
Trey, 61
W., 83
Wilmer F., 61
Himol
H., 59
Hines
Geo. Thos, 68
H. B., 68
Hinson
Rose, 12
Hitchings
Louisa, 112
Lucy, 112
Hodge
Thos, 35
Hodges
B., 42
Bertha, 56
C. L., 99
E. E., 2
mamie, 101
Mrs. H., 87
N. S., 98

S. B., 99
Hogan
Pearl, 55
Hogans
L. J., 58
Holland
Leone, 13
Mary, 106
Holloway
Abram, 53
Allice, 53
Holly
C. H., 17
Holmes
Alice D., 11
Mary, 90
Sarah, 26
Holms
Celia, 55
Holt
David, 91
Holtzclaw
Jas., 82
Hook
Hendrick, 4
Hoon
S., 28
Hooper
L., 81
Hopkins
C. L., 83
C. W., 34
Green B., 53
Hopson
S. A. E., 97
Horrell
Eddy, 63
Shelby, 63
House, 28
Howard
Cordelia, 106
Dennis, 28
Henderson, 49
Henry, 49
John W., 106
Martha, 105

Index

Hubbard
  F. D., 99
Hudnall
  mac, 30
Huggins
  J. A., 39
  M. C., 39
Hughes
  Alice G., 109
Hughey
  Susan, 79
Hull, 95
  Belle, 85
  Mertie, 95
Humbolt
  Annie, 120
Humphrey
  Anne, 65
  Chester, 65
Humphreys
  M. P., 97
Humphries
  Daniel, 54
  S. C., 24
H(unreadable
  B., 31
H(unreadable)
  Gail, 48
Hunter
  Alexander, 88
  Ann, 56
  E., 71
  Fannie, 88
  Frank, 11
  James, 102
  M., 43
  M. C., 102
  M. L., 103
  R., 33
  William, 33
Hurst
  Martha, 55
Husdon
  Wm. G., 6
Hutson
  Juley, 48

Hutto
  Ola Bell, 55
Hyder
  Wm., 8

I

ickinson
  Fredonia, 62
Inent
  Illa, 5
Infant
  O. M., 3
Ingraham
  Cathernise, 118
  Infant, 77
Ingram
  E. M., 32
Inmes
  Mrs. L., 92

J

Jackman
  Frank, 80
Jackson
  Abe, 22
  Brian, 50
  F., 20
  Fanny, 107
  Handy, 110
  Henry, 51
  Hessie, 54
  Jesse E., 30
  John, 88
  Lewis, 54
  Louis, 92
  Mary, 27
  Silla, 102
  Thos., 87
Janny
  Eva, 82
Jeems
  Randall, 108
Jeffrey
  Benj, 75
Jenkins
  Ella, 104

Hannah, 73
  Mary, 73
  Phoebe, 17
  Willie, 88
Jensko
  Ladny Patsy, 88
Jerkins
  Sophy, 47
Jernigan
  Callie, 119
  Jesse, 92
Jinkins
  Kate, 13
John
  Jerry, 3
Johns
  C. I., 31
  Luke, 91
  W. R., 33
Johnson
  A. H., 33
  Annie, 112
  Baby, 60
  Bill, 108
  Brutus, 70
  Clint, 103
  D., 41
  Elizabeth, 9
  El(unreadable), 116
  Fleming, 69
  H. Julia, 43
  Henry, 16
  Infant (of Samuel Johnson), 78
  Ira, 32
  Isaac, 9
  Jas., 107
  John, 41
  Ladie, 69
  Laura F., 85
  Lizzie, 69
  Louisa, 53
  Maria, 110
  Martha, 64
  Mary, 86
  Mary E., 120

13

Index

Index

Laird
  B. F., 110
Lake
  James, 107
Lakeman(?)
  Anthony, 10
Lambert
  O. J., 25
Lamm
  Freonia, 60
Lanairs
  Lizzie, 87
Land
  Andrew, 32
  Jno., 14
  Sarah, 40
Landin
  Nellie, 9
Lane
  Mary, 102
Lanell
  Clara, 21
  M. L., 21
Langford
  G. W., 66
Langnord
  Hugh, 7
Lanier, 99
  Alice E., 99
  Laura M., 99
Lannie
  Lewis, 84
Larkins
  B. M., 98
Larry
  Amy, 36
Lasseter
  A. V., 101
Lattermore
  Cha., 81
Launi
  Ed. N., 75
Laures
  Jose, 121
Law
  Patty, 59

Lawler
  Alexander, 92
  Mrs. Michael, 94
Lawson
  Lue, 11
Leake
  Esther, 17
Leavins
  Elijah, 39
Ledwitch
  Wm. F. (infant), 113
Lee
  Catharine, 81
  Eliza, 63
  Gracy, 87
  Infant, 56
  Lizzie, 68
  Marrion, 81
  Pearl, 60
  Sarah, 99
  T. V., 80
Leek
  Geo., 108
Leggins
  Robert, 90
  William, 90
Legree
  Jossey, 23
  Wm. T., 23
Leitner
  M. H., 73
Lennent
  S. E., 38
Leon
  Fidelia, 114
  Robert, 53
  Theodore, 114
Leonous
  Sallie, 82
Leslie
  Sue, 67
Levy
  H. C., 53
  John S., 110
Lewis
  Eugena, 100

Hattie, 58
  Julia, 44
  Lula, 94
  Susan, 22
Lightsey
  D. E., 44
Lilins
  H. J., 91
Lilly
  E., 103
Linder
  L., 74
Lindsey
  Mariah, 53
Lines
  Charles, 120
Linton
  M. A., 45
  Rebecca, 112
  Roxey, 112
Livingston
  Cope, 95
  S. H., 62
  Tom, 68
Loid
  Juana, 79
Long
  Solan, 87
  Willie, 67
Lopez
  Eloyse, 93
  Hattie, 93
  Mrs. D., 93
  Rufina, 121
Louis
  R., 8
Love
  Ann, 27
  M. J., 25
  M. M., 96
Lovelace
  Martha, 90
  Susan, 87
Lovett
  Andrew, 49
Lowe

15

Index

McDavid, 48
McDonald
  George J., 113
  Jos., 81
  Joseph E., 118
  N., 15
McEashem, 98
McEntyre
  Stella, 65
McGehee
  Ella, 97
McGurie
  G. H., 45
McHeugh
  P., 16
McI (?)
  Ethel W., 102
McIlwane
  W., 57
McIntire
  Dilsey, 68
McKeeson
  Catherine, 79
McKinley
  Elizabeth, 119
McKinney
  J. T., 93
  Jacob, 70
  Olive, 70
McKinny
  Sam, 46
McKinzay
  Grace, 108
  Nathan, 108
  Ruford, 108
McLanry
  Susan, 88
McLean
  C. S., 107
  Flora, 111
  John, 107
McLeary
  Maggie, 62
McLellan
  Babe, 91
McLendon

Jm., 98
McLeod
  Dan, 88
  Juda, 86
mcLeod
  Max, 111
  Wm., 112
McLin
  P. N., 37
  R. M., 37
McManna
  Mary J., 102
McMullan
  A. A., 4
McMullen
  Gehazu J., 112
McNeal
  H. W., 26
McNealy
  E. L., 40
McQuaig
  Baby, 79
McRae
  Sallie, 15
  W. E., 90
McWilliams
  J. R., 109
Meacham
  Bill, 110
  James, 110
Meadly
  Jas., 23
Medlin
  R. L., 115
Med(unreadable)
  M. A., 31
Meegan
  Jas, 9
Meeks
  L., 103
Mench
  Annie Eliza, 74
Menz
  Manuel, 121
Mercer
  Julia, 71

  Rosanna, 110
Merides
  Manuel, 123
Mesena
  Cornelia, 74
Messina
  Magella, 24
Mickler
  Jackson, 93
Micle(Michael)
  Jacob, 72
Mikles
  Henry, 41
Milam
  L. B., 99
Mile
  Robt. H., 81
Miles
  Ed., 8
Millen
  B., 33
  C., 33
Miller
  C. V., 99
  Chas, 69
  Ed, 29
  Emilu, 88
  Emmaline, 110
  Hattie, 13
  Jno, 69
  john, 17
  John, 111
  Lizzetta, 48
  Mrs. J., 86
  Robert, 17
  U. U., 13
  V., 12
  William, 29
Millian, 79
Mills
  G. M., 84
  W. W., 2
Minich
  Jimme A., 36
Minor
  L. A., 84

17

Index

Index

Index

Index

Index

Index

Alfred, 18
Tonis
  Juan, 116
Tooke
  Caro, 67
  J.. B., 58
  Lotty, 67
Tossis
  Fernando, 123
Townsend
  Sarah, 66
Tran
  Ejaos, 122
Trask
  Georgia E., 85
Trulock
  Anna, 25
  G. L., 25
Truman
  Florida, 67
Tryon
  Marvin, 35
Tucker
  A. A., 86
  Chas. P., 94
  J. W. L., 86
  Jim, 34
  Millard, 62
  Peter, 62
  W. L., 86
Tully
  george E., 120
Tumblin
  Hardy, 4
Turnage
  W. R., 95
Turner
  Frank, 12
  George, 49
  M. T., 59
  N., 85
  W. H., 85
  Wm. H., 18
Tuten
  Julia, 33
  Mary H., 65

Tyner
  Ailcey M., 58
  Susan, 58
  W. K., 80
Tynner, 59

U

Ugarte
  Petronia, 121
Underhill
  Jerry, 2
Ungh
  Ruth, 99
Union
  Aaron, 20
Updyke
  Manuel, 94
Uriola
  Rafael, 120
Usher
  Hezekiah, 69

V

Valac
  Amelia, 113
Valdes
  Elvida, 118
Valdez
  Gregorio, 120
  Simian, 78
Vaneta
  Sofia, 75
Varnes
  Julia, 91
Vaughn
  Bell, 20
Veach
  John W., 80
Vendick
  Chas., 8
Ventura
  Elias, 74
Vialeh
  Felix, 77
Vickers
  Rayford, 109

Vicus
  Bessa, 48
VilyAguero
  Luisa, 118
Virgil
  Robert, 16
Vogel
  Horace, 18
Von PFuler(?)
  Wm. H., 75

W

Wade
  Agnes, 16
  Irene, 15
  Jn, 57
  (unreadable), 15
Wagner
  Alex, 87
  Frank, 14
  Herman, 76
Waite
  Flopey (or Flossy), 120
Walden
  Chas., 12
  Joe, 12
Walker
  Alfred, 7
  Amanda, 44
  Arthur, 64
  Audrey V., 119
  Benj., 64
  Chas., 26
  John, 64
  M. M., 100
  Mabel, 8
Walking
  Nellie, 100
Wall
  L. W., 8
Wallace
  Lillian, 123
  Margaret, 122
Waller
  Infant, 57
Walls

Index

Index

Adner, 20
Williams, 29
  Alice W., 97
  Baby, 60
  Chas., 6
  Cornelius, 90
  David, 53
  E., 59
  E. S., 33
  Ed, 67
  Eliza, 55
  Ellen, 87
  Florence, 28
  Florinda, 9
  Francis, 11
  Frank, 54
  H. P., 32
  Hiram E., 111
  Infant, 57
  J. A. J., 38
  J. L., 9
  Jno., 12
  Jnoy., 11
  Joe, 39
  Johnny, 5
  Julia W., 43
  Laura, 50
  Lettie, 30
  Liza, 13
  Lizzie, 46
  Martha, 67
  Mary, 67
  May, 30
  Mrs. Robert, 22
  Peter, 96
  Priscilla, 51
  R., 57
  Rachel, 50
  Robert, 52
  Robt., 18
  Ross, 34
  Samm, 94
  Sophia H., 120
  Tim, 67
  Willie, 10
  Wm., 107

Williams, Sr.
  Robert, 27
Williamson, 94
Willie
  Prod, 83
Willis
  B., 3
  Henry, 97
  Laura, 44
Willson
  Clara, 23
Wilsa
  Caroline G., 119
Wilson
  Abram, 15
  Charity, 52
  Clifford, 51
  E. Maria, 25
  George, 72
  Jesse, 40
  John, 58
  Laura, 118
  Mary, 42
  Mr., 71
  Phoebe, 60
  Sarah A., 88
Wimberly
  Maggie, 81
Winans
  Jns., 57
Wing
  P., 93
Wingate
  Jonathan, 35
Winkaman
  Johanna, 82
Witherspoon
  Mucky, 24
Wood
  B, 84
  Lollie S., 4
  Lorine, 80
  margaret, 22
  May P., 4
  Paul, 4
Woodberry

  D., 29
Woodrough
  Grace L., 80
  Martha, 81
Woods
  Louisa, 101
  Mary, 106
Woodward
  Baby, 52
  Mach, 52
Wright
  A., 46
  Alexander, 121
  B., 103
  Henry, 18, 114
  J., 103
  Louisa, 114
  N., 103
  Samuel, 105
Wyman
  C. W., 1
Wynn
  Baby, 40
  Wm. H., 58

Y

Yates
  Jackson, 4
  Sarah, 74
Yates, Jr.
  James, 37
Yeates
  Mattie, 77
Yeomans
  Susanna, 54
Yon
  Isaac, 24
York
  Martha, 106
Young, 97
  Baby, 18
  John, 100
  Lily, 9
  Lucy, 72
  Margaret, 68
  Mary, 18

ABOUT THE AUTHOR

Alvie L. Davidson retired from Naval Intelligence in the U.S. Naval Reserve after twenty-two years of service. Since then he has been a Florida state licensed private investigator, specializing in missing persons and genealogical applications of investigations. He is the past District Director of the Florida Association of Licensed Investigators and recognized by the Circuit Court of numerous Florida counties as an expert in the field of Probate Investigation.

Alvie is certified as a CG (Certified Genealogist) by the Board for Certification of Genealogists, Washington, DC. He is an alumni of the National Institute on Genealogical Research, Washington, DC (1998); and the Institute of Genealogy & Historical Research, Samford University, Birmingham, Alabama (1999 and 2000). He is the founder (1981) and President of the Imperial Polk Genealogical Society, Lakeland, Florida.

He has served on the Board of Directors of the Association of Professional Genealogists for ten years as a director.

Alvie is author of *Florida Land: Records of the Tallahassee and Newnansville Federal Land Office, 1826-1892* (Heritage Books, Bowie, MD 1988) and has published articles in *The Genealogical Helper*. He has lived most of his adult life in Central Florida, currently residing at 4825 North Galloway Road, Lakeland, Florida.

Additional information can be found at http://www.floridadetective.net.

www.ingramcontent.com/pod-product-compliance
Lightning Source LLC
Chambersburg PA
CBHW072254270326
41930CB00010B/2373